A SPIRITUAL
AUTOBIOGRAPHY

WILLIAM B. EERDMANS PUBLISHING COMPANY

©William Barclay 1975
First Published 1975 by A. R. Mowbray & Co. Ltd.,
under the title TESTAMENT OF FAITH.
This edition published by special arrangement
with A. R. Mowbray & Co. Ltd.

Library of Congress Cataloging in Publication Data

Barclay, William, lecturer in the University of Glasgow.
A spirtual autobiography.

 1.   Barclay, William, lecturer in the University of
Glasgow.   I.   Title.
BS2351.B28A37   230'.092'4[B]   73-76528
ISBN 0-8028-3464-7

Printed in the United States of America

CONTENTS

I

THIS FOR REMEMBRANCE

If ever I am going to write a book which sets forth my 'testament of faith', now is the time to do so. Very recently I received my old age pension papers. At a conference of doctors a short time ago those attending were divided into groups, and I found myself allocated to the geriatric section. A year from the time I am writing this I will be retiring from my job in the University of Glasgow. One morning last week, after a lecture, I was carefully putting the pages of my manuscript back into their folder. I was straightening them up so that the edges would be level and so that the paper would not be creased, and I found myself saying to myself: 'What does it matter? I won't be using them again anyway.' These days I have the odd sensation of doing things for the last time. Somerset Maugham wrote in his autobiography, *The Summing Up*: 'When I have finished this book, I shall know where I stand. I can afford then to do what I choose with the years that remain to me.' *I shall know where I stand* — at my age I ought to know where I stand. As he grew older H. G. Wells used to say that he felt as he used to feel when he was a child and his nurse said: 'Master George, it's time to put your toys away.' Indeed, it is time to put the toys away and to see just where I stand. It is a good time to look back across life and to ask what the things are by which I have lived.

Visser 't Hooft begins his *Memoirs* by telling how one of his children returned a book, borrowed from his library, with the comment: 'I do not like it. It is an I-book.' If a man has to set down his testament of faith, he cannot avoid talking about himself, because what he most surely believes depends on what he is and what life has done to him. There is no one in the world harder to write about than oneself. Margot Asquith has an unidentified quotation in one of her books: 'A well written life is almost as rare as a well spent one.' If that is true of lives, it is even truer of autobiographies. The old Greek sages said: 'Know yourself.' It is not a question of honesty or of self-deception; it is just that it is very difficult—perhaps impossible—for any man to know himself. But if a man is to talk about his beliefs, he cannot avoid talking about himself, and so there is no point in wasting time apologising for a necessity.

I think that it was Heine who said that a man cannot be too careful in the choice of his parents, and certainly I was fortunate in mine. Alexander Scott in *Still Life*, the biography of William Soutar, the Scottish poet, quotes Soutar as saying: 'If I have been privileged to catch a more comprehensive glimpse of life than many other men, it is because I have stood on the shoulders of my parents.' I have to make the acknowledgement without making the claim. I can make no claim to having had 'a more comprehensive glimpse of life' than other men. But, whatever I have done in life, it is because 'I have stood on the shoulders of my parents', and to this day there are places in Scotland where I am still my father's son—and I am glad that it is so.

My father, William Dugald Barclay, was a Gaelic-speaking highlander, born in Fort William and buried in Kilmallie, which looks across Loch Linnhe to Ben Nevis. He was a bank agent, or, as it is now more grandly called, a bank manager. He married late, and I was a late child. He married late for the simple reason that after eighteen years in the service of the bank his salary had reached £80 a year. He was appointed to his first agency in Wick in 1905 at a salary of £120 a year and no house. He married then, and I was born in Wick, in 1907.

My father had no advanced education, but he had the best library I have ever seen in the possession of a layman, and he was a notable preacher. He was not a lay reader or anything like that; he never took a penny piece for preaching, not even his travelling expenses; but later, between 1912 and 1929, when we were in Motherwell—I think my figures are right—he preached in thirteen out of Motherwell's then fourteen churches.

I do not want to give a wrong impression. My father was no saint. Many years later a doctor, who was also something of a psychologist, was to ask me—I have no idea why: 'At what age did you discover that your father was fallible?' I never thought him anything else but fallible. He had an explosive temper, but it was like fire in straw. It blazed and died, and he never remembered it, and did not expect anyone else to remember it. A stranger would have thought that he and I lived at war—but we didn't—we were friends. Surely the greatest kind of friendship is when you can differ with some one to the point of violence and yet remain united in heart.

It must have been from my father that I learned the love of games that has stayed with me all my life. He a was little man, and he carried weight, but I remember to this day the football 'matches' we played on the hillside above Fort William in the holiday days. I remember the golf we played in Hamilton every week. He had in his youth been a notable shinty player. (With apologies to the highlanders, I should explain that shinty is a kind of primitive hockey.) He played golf as if it was shinty. I don't suppose he ever hit the ball more than a hundred-and-fifty yards. But I doubt if he was ever off the fairway in all his playing days.

So, when I was majestically dispatching the ball large distances to all the point of the compass except the right one, he would give it three sharp raps up the fairway on to the green and sink the putt. As we left the tee, he for the middle of the fairway, I for the wilds, he would say smugly: 'See you at the green!' and go on his undeviating way. I thereby learned the useful lesson that, however far you go, it is not much use if it is not in the right direction. I remember on one of the rare occasions when we were in London together he took me to the Oval, and we saw Jack Hobbs out for 96 to Joe Hulme in the last over of the day, as he tried to hit a four to get his hundred before stumps were drawn.

The generation gap was there all right. Even when I was quite grown up there were explosive rackets about when I came in at night—or rather in the morning. He was highlander enough to have more than half a suspicion that dancing was sinful. But somehow it never spoiled things. When I went to be a parish minister in Renfrew, after my mother died, he lived alone, looked after by the faithful Rebecca who had been our housekeeper for twenty years and more. He would never come and make his home with me—he was far too wise for that, but there was never a night when we did not phone each other. We fought to the end of the day—we fought—for my theology was if anything even more to be suspected than my dancing; but for all that we were friends.

I remember G. K. Chesterton, in one of his books, telling how when he was a child, he had a toy theatre. One of the cardboard figures was a man with a great golden key. Chesterton said that he had long since forgotten what character the man with the key represented, but somehow he always associated this man with his father, because his father had unlocked for him so many doors to wonderful things—and I too can say that of my father.

4

My mother—she was the nearest approach to a saint I ever knew. She *was* a saint—not just nearly one. Tall, fair, blue-eyed, gracious, beautiful, every inch an aristocrat, she was the daughter of Colonel Daniel McLeish of Parade House, Fort William. My father was the son of the village joiner—and there was opposition to the wedding. She could write, she could paint, she could play the piano, but above all she was kind, and, when all the guns were blazing at home, she was the buffer and the peace-maker between my father and me.

To the modern generation J. M. Barrie is an out-of-date sentimentalist, but he still moves me. I remember what he wrote about his mother in *Margaret Ogilvy*:

When you looked into my mother's eyes you knew, as if He had told you, why God sent her into the world—it was to open the minds of all who looked to beautiful thoughts.

The time was to come when at school and university distinctions and successes were to come to me. I can quite honestly say that it made no difference to me, but it pleased her—and that made a difference to me. Isobel Field tells how one day she found Robert Louis Stevenson turning over the pages of a scrap-book his mother had kept with notices about him in the papers and reviews of his books and the like. She said to him jestingly: 'Is fame all it's cracked up to be?' 'Yes,' he answered, 'when I see my mother's face.' Any successes which came to me are not in the same world as the successes which came to Stevenson— but I know and understand what he meant. Edward Marsh in his autobiography tells of his mother's death, and then goes on: 'A week or two afterwards I learned that I had passed second in the Civil Service examination: and I realised that the person in the world who cared most what

5

happened to me was gone for ever.' Nothing was every the same when she was not there to tell it to.

She died in 1932 of cancer of the spine, an agonising death—and left me facing the theological problem that to this day I have never solved. Why should my mother, lovely in body and in spirit, good all through, have to die like that? She died just when I was being licensed as a preacher. 'You'll have a new note in your preaching now,' my father said to me through his own tears—and so I had—not the note of one who knew the answers and had solved the problems, but the note of one who now knew what the problems were. The last thing she ever gave me was a soft leather sermon case—and from that day to this, more than forty years later, I never went into a pulpit without it. I thank God on every remembrance of my mother.

It is a good thing to set one's faith in the light of one's debts. Marcus Aurelius begins his *Meditations* with eight pages of the acknowledgement of his debts to those who had made him what he was. I want to do the same.

Outside the home the first world with which we all come into contact is school. We came to Motherwell in 1912, when I was five. It was there I went to school. At first the schooling was much interrupted, because for me the change from the clean air of Wick to the smoke of Motherwell, and the emergence from the protection of home to the exposure to the world, resulted in six illnesses in five years—diphtheria, scarlet fever, measles, jaundice, chickenpox, whooping-cough. It turned out all to the good, for in the enforced absences from school even then I learned to read for myself, and learned more miscellaneous knowledge than school could ever have taught me.

I was lucky in my school. It was Dalziel High School (pronounced D L) in Motherwell, just an ordinary school, no fees or anything like that, comprehensive long before that word was ever used, a complete cross-section of the community, Scottish education at its best. To this day the members of my old school class meet to dine together once a year, and out of that one school class there sit down to dinner every November two headmasters, three doctors, the general manager of one of Scotland's greatest steel works, a Glasgow bank manager, a lawyer, a county director of education, the principal clerk of the General Assembly of the Church of Scotland, and two professors.

In Dalziel High we got more than just book-learning. There was football, cricket, tennis, athletics, golf, swimming; and—maybe best of all—every year the school produced a Gilbert and Sullivan opera. In the unlikely event of the operas getting lost I can supply them all— words and music—from memory. It was magnificent schooling, because it meant that, if a boy or girl in Dalziel High had any kind of talent, in any kind of sphere, he or she was going to get the chance and the encouragement to use it. I loved my school and still do. It is not just because I see my school days in a golden haze that I look back on them as the happiest days in life. I know what Barrie meant when he said: 'The horror of my childhood was that I knew a time must come when I also must give up the games, and how it was to be done I saw not.' It was not just the games; it was that whole life of community which was never fully to be experienced again.

Dalziel High had a magnificent staff of teachers, but to three of them my debt is great. There was Geordie Robertson who taught me Latin and Greek for five years. The day was to come when I was to graduate with first-class honours in Classics and I would have liked to take that degree and lay it at Geordie's feet. Geordie was one of the old school, indeed the vanished school. The extraordinary thing about him was that he himself had no degree at all. Nowadays he would not even have been allowed to teach in a Senior Secondary School; far less could he have become the head of a department. But no one could ever have put the rudiments of Latin and Greek into his pupils like Geordie. W. B. Yeats tells of a certain Bishop Grundtvig who was the pioneer of Danish education. He says of him that he educated Denmark 'by making examinations almost nothing and the personality of the teacher almost everything'. Geordie was the perfect demonstration of the fact that not only preaching but also teaching is 'truth through personality'. Surely it is one of the supreme achievements of life to open to others doors through which we never passed ourselves—and Geordie did just that. And yet Geordie was a teacher whom modern efficiency would simply have eliminated—and that may well be what is wrong with modern teaching.

There is—not was—A. D. Robertson, for A.D. is still alive and very much with us. It was from 1922 to 1925 that he taught us, fifty years ago, and he still attends our annual dinner looking younger and fresher than the people he taught half a century ago. He was every inch a scholar and he taught us to love English literature and to love the English language; he opened to us the magic of words, and this is a magic which, once it has laid its grip upon you, will never let you go. H. A. L. Fisher, in *An Unfinished Autobiography*, described how his father read aloud Greek poetry to his sons:

> From my own experience I should doubt whether any part of education can be so valuable to a child as that he should hear soon and often the great masterpieces of poetry from the lips of someone who feels their beauty and can transmit it.

A.D., somehow or other, communicated to us his own love for the beautiful.

A great teacher has the undefinable something. Edwin Muir in his autobiography wrote of Miss Annan who in

Kirkwall taught him English when he was a lad. She did not use the strap at all—she did not need to.

> She had a cheerful, impudent, devoted class, who only needed her presence to become inspired. She taught us English, and but for her we might never have realised what the subject meant beyond the drudgery of parsing and analysis. She opened out eyes; we felt we were a sort of aristocracy, for what we did for her we did freely. She must have been a remarkable woman; she seemed to have endless charm, vitality and patience. She filled us with confidence and a kind of goodness which was quite unlike the goodness asked from us by the other teachers. Yet she never put us on our honour; she simply took us as we were and by some power changed us.

That might well have been written of A.D. A teacher who has taught his scholars to love literature has given them something which will do far more than enable them to pass examinations—he has given them a joy for ever.

There was Jimmy Paterson—Monkey Brand they called him. He had served in the Royal Scots Fusiliers in the First World War—some said he was the regimental sergeant major. After the war he took a brilliant first in Classics, and then he came to Dalziel High, when I was beginning my sixth year—and he changed my life. Until then I was going to the university to read English; but Jimmy made me fall in love with Greek. He was a magnificent teacher. He and I would go up to the tower room after four o'clock, and we would read Greek, exploring the *Iliad* 'far on the ringing plains of windy Troy', listening to 'the surge and thunder of the *Odssey*'. To A.D. I owe the love of the English language which has been the delight of a life-time; to Jimmy Paterson I owe that love of Greek which was to give me my life-work. It has been well said that there are two kinds of education—one teaches us how to make a living and the other teaches us how to live—and it was the glory of Dalziel High that it carried out both kinds of education admirably well.

And so in 1925 I arrived in Glasgow University to read Classics—and once again I was blessed in my teachers. There was McNeile Dixon, Professor of English and Rhetoric, with his monocle and his Irish brogue, the scholar who in *The Human Situation* gave what I suppose is the only series of Gifford Lectures which, issued in a book, became a best-seller, and which anyone could understand! In *Moral Philosophy* there was A. A. Bowman, destined to die all too soon, and pouring out with a kind of superb and reckless generosity the few years that remained to him. In Greek there was Gilbert Austin Davies, the most fastidious and meticulous scholar I have ever met. And above all there was John Swinnerton Phillimore in Latin, or Humanity, as it was officially known. All kinds of people from all kinds of classes came to hear Phillimore lecture. He would come in and he would stand. In those days university classes sang—how they sang! For some reason Glasgow University classes sang 'Ye Mariners of England', and sang it with gusto and even with beauty. So we sang that, and Phillimore still benignly waited. And then the class—close on three-hundred of them—would sing to the tune of 'There is a better world above':

> O Phillimore, we love you so,
> Yes we do, yes we do!

Or sometimes when we were in contrary mood:

> O Phillimore, we love you well,
> Do we hell, do we hell!

Then, having been sung to, Phillimore would give a hitch to his gown and embark on Terence to a fascinated class.

I shall never forget the last time I saw him. I had won a

prize in his class, and I went to his house to settle what book I was to get. He was kindness itself, giving his whole attention to his student. I did not know then that in an hour's time he was to go for the train which was to take him to hospital for that operation for cancer from which he died. There was surely unparalleled courtesy in the heart of the man who gave all of himself to a student an hour before he was to go out to die. There was Bill Rennie who started in Greek, moved to Latin to succeed Phillimore, and then moved back to Greek. He was a pugnacious, belligerent creature, but he loved his classics. I have seen him for a whole hour march up and down, not his rostrum, but the passages of the classroom pouring out the translation— without any comment at all—of a whole book of the *Iliad*, drunk with the beauty of the Greek and intoxicated with the sonorous English of which he was such a master. There were giants in those days, and it was God's gift to me that— even if only at a distance—I knew them.

So in 1929 I arrived in Trinity College, Glasgow, the United Free Church College, to begin the final stage of training for the ministry—and once again I was supremely fortunate in my teachers.

There was W. D. Niven who taught Church History. Niven was one of the last of the polymaths. He was, so to speak, a philosopher by trade, for it was with honours in philosophy that he graduated. He became Professor of Church History; he later moved over to teach New Testament; and before he was finished he returned to Church History. Some one said of him that what W. D. Niven needed to occupy was not a professor's chair but a settee! There was J. E. McFadyen, Professor of Old Testament, a man of immense learning combined with childlike simplicity. He had married a German wife whom he had met during his studies in Marburg, and he used to say that the only cure for the world's ills was for every man to marry a wife of another nationality. He used to go to hear students preach—without warning. He arrived one evening in a church in which the student who was preaching was about to preach one of Johnnie's own sermons! The wretched student was too inexperienced to switch; he had to go ahead. After the service Johnnie appeared in the vestry. The student was ready to sink through the floor but Johnnie came forward with both hands outstretched and shining eyes. 'Mr So-and-so,' he said, 'thank you—thank you—for doing me the honour of preaching one of my sermons'—and it was said in all sincerity. He followed the college football team. At a certain match one of the lads was quite badly hurt. That lad was the assistant in charge of a little mission in a slum part of Glasgow. That night Johnnie was at that lad's door. 'Mr So-and-so,' he said, 'could I take your mission services on Sunday, if you are not able to take them yourself?' Johnnie was laden with academic honours, but if ever any man had the childlike spirit, he had. No wonder his students loved him—and to teach Hebrew and to be loved is no mean achievement!

There was A. B. Macaulay, a great theologian, but so tense and nervous that he had to retire all too young from what was for him the intolerable burden of teaching. I was very close to him, partly because I was so indecipherable a hand-writer that he had to send for me to read my examination papers aloud to him. He sent for me a day or two before I was due to leave college. 'Willie,' he said, 'do you mind if I say something to you?' 'Certainly not,' I said. 'Well then,' he said, 'I want to say this to you—if you don't get rid of that Glasgow accent you will never get anywhere in the Church!' I didn't get rid of it. The day came when I had to do some talking on television! I often go into a shop and, when I give my order, some one says: 'Ah! I recognize that voice!' A Scots voice with what some one called a sound like gravel has become a trade-mark.

There was A. J. Gossip, one of the world's supreme preachers, who taught us Practical Training. Gossip lived closer to God than any man I have ever known. At one time he was minister of St Matthew's in Glasgow. I have heard him tell how there was a week when pressure of all kinds of things made it difficult to make the preparation he knew he should have made. 'You know the stair up to the pulpit in St Matthew's?' he said. 'You know the bend on the stair? Jesus Christ met me there. I saw him as clearly as I see you. He looked at the sermon in my hand. "Gossip," he said to me, "is this the best you could do for me this week?"' and Gossip went on: 'Thinking back over the business of that week, I could honestly say: "Yes, Lord, it is my best".' And said Gossip: 'Jesus Christ took that poor thing that Sunday morning and in his hands it became a trumpet.' And somehow, when you knew Gossip, it seemed quite natural that he should meet and talk with Jesus.

There was W. M. Macgregor, who taught the New Testament. This man had more influence on me than anyone outside my home. He was a difficult character. A saturnine character with, I think, a not undeliberately calculated resemblance to Dante, a man of terrible silences, a man with a tongue dipped in vitriol. 'Who,' said a friend of his, 'can stand before his cold?' And yet a man with a sudden smile like the sun breaking across a wintry sky, a shy man, but a man for all his external awesomeness with a heart amazingly kind. In an article on him Gossip spoke of Macgregor's 'prodigious and Christ-like memory'. He gives one instance. 'Well, John,' Macgregor greeted a student on his first day in college, 'and how is your sister Margaret? She must be nineteen now,' 'Yes, sir.' 'And James, he'll be seventeen.' 'Yes, sir, but how do you know, sir.' 'Why, lad, I spent a night in your father's manse when I was Moderator!' One night—all of fifteen years ago—in a year when he was in two or three different manses every week—and the names and the ages graven on his memory. 'There is something,' says Gossip, 'almost God-like about that!'

Macgregor himself was a student of A. B. Bruce, that great New Testament scholar who stamped Glasgow with the tradition it has had ever since. Macgregor said of Bruce: 'He cut the cables and gave us a glimpse of the blue waters.' Macgregor did that for me. When Macgregor was called to his chair, some people were surprised he should leave the pulpit and the congregation where he had done so much and go to teach. He answered that he had learned some things from A. B. Bruce that he would like to pass on. And when I, his pupil, was called to my work in Glasgow, I too could say that I had learned some few things from W. M. Macgregor that I wanted to pass on. Gossip ends his article on W. M. Macgregor with this quotation: ' "I do not know", wrote Principle John Cairns to his teacher Sir William Hamilton, "what life, or lives, may lie before me. But this I know that, to the end of the last of them, I shall bear your mark upon me".' I can say that of W. M. Macgregor.

Of two people I must still speak. The first is G. H. C. Macgregor, my predecessor in the New Testament chair in Glasgow. I was his lecturer for seventeen years. I never knew a man who was at one and the same time so much the mystic and the scholar. He was never strong. Throughout the years I came to love him. I went to see him in his last illness to tell him not to worry, that all was well with the department. He was a highlander with the Gaelic, and high-landers—I am one myself—can say things that lowlanders would shrink from saying. I did not know I was not to see him again, and as I left his bedroom, he put his hand on mine and said: 'Willie, when I die they'll find your name written on my heart.' In one of Socrates' scenes Socrates asked a simple old man for what he was most thankful, for what he most wanted to thank God, and the old man answered: 'That being such as I am I have had the friends I have had.' And as I look back that is exactly how I feel.

I have left the greatest of all my debts to the end. I married Kate in June 1933, and I cannot think what life would have been without her. She is not one of those wives who go out working; she has made a whole-time job of looking after me and our children and our grandchildren— and I am sure she was right. Barrie in *Margaret Ogilvy* talks of what happened in Kirriemuir when he was a boy. Until that time the main industry had been weaving at home. Each house had its loom and the man of the house did the weaving. Then the machine came and the factories opened up. It was young people the power-looms needed and bit by bit the men were left with nothing to do, but the mills were filled with the girls. Among them were young wives who had gone out to work. Barrie writes:

> With so many of the family, young mothers among them, working in the factories, home life is not so beautiful as it was. So much of what is great in Scotland has sprung from the closeness of the family ties; it is there I sometimes fear my country is being struck.

It may be that wives have to work for the money that is needed; it may be that they have to work to express themselves in something other than the work of a housewife— but I wonder. I would hate a home where in the morning both husband and wife were under the pressures of getting out in time. Still more I would hate a home with no one there when I come home. And if I an adult would hate it, how much more a child? I cannot really see how anyone can run a job and a home.

My wife is not an academic; I doubt if she has ever read a book that I have written! She is no weakling as a critic. It has been said—and truly—that only two people can and will tell you the truth, an enemy who hates you bitterly and a friend who loves you dearly. I think that my wife has all our married life kept me from pride. I am certain that the worst thing a man could have is a doting wife for whom her husband can do no wrong. But I have noticed that, although my wife is my sternest critic, she will defend me against those outside the family who criticise me. The astringent quality of her attitude to my performance has always been a prophylactic against conceit!

Kate's father was the minister of the parish of Dundonald in Ayrshire for the better part of fifty years, and so, when I was in a parish, there was nothing she could not do. She has all the qualities which I do not possess. I am a handless creature. Like Hilaire Belloc

> A lost thing I could never find,
> Nor a broken thing mend.

I am an untidy character. Domestically, I am helpless. And I have been looked after, cared for, protected all my life.

As I look back on more than forty years of married life, I am astonished that the work of the ministry does not destroy ministers' marriages. The minister will have the best and the biggest room in the house for his study. The minister sees less of his family than any member of his congregation does. He sees less of his children. He has to leave it to his wife to bring them up. Seldom can he have an evening out with his wife and, even when such an evening is arranged, something again and again comes to stop it. Demands to speak and to lecture take him constantly away from home and, when he does come home, he is so tired that he is the worst company in the world, and falls asleep in his chair. As I come near to the end of my days, the one thing that haunts me more than anything else is that I have been so unsatisfactory a husband and a father. As the Song of Solomon has it: 'They made me keeper of the vineyards; but my own vineyard I have not kept.' When the Pastoral Epistles are laying down the qualifications for the elder, the deacon and the bishop one of the unvarying demands is that 'he must know how to manage his own household'—and for a minister that is the hardest thing in the world.

I do not know the answer to this. The ministry is a twenty-four hour in the day job, for the minister has to be always on call, whenever trouble may strike a home in his congregation. That is why there can never be a part-time ministry. If a minister is sent for he cannot arrange that a message be sent: 'I'll come when I get back from work at six o'clock.' By that time it may well be too late. I am all for women in the ministry, but I would write it in that a woman should resign her charge if and when she marries. A woman cannot have babies and a congregation. One or the other is going to suffer. Sermons to write every morning, people to visit every afternoon, meetings to attend in the evening— when is the baby to be fed, when are the children to be bathed, when is the restless unhappy child to be sung to and cuddled to sleep, when is the family to be loved? By all means women in the ministry—but not the ministry *and* marriage, for both are whole-time jobs.

I once before said these things in print, and a minister wrote in and said that he had trained his congregation never to call on his services on a Monday. I suppose he must have had an arrangement with God that no one in his congregation died on a Monday, that no home was stricken with some tragedy, that no one needed God. There are some things which will not wait; if they are not done now they cannot be done at all.

As I have said I don't know the answer to this. I do not know how Kate has put up with me for forty years. All I know is that I have been cared for and protected for all my days with a care and a protection which no man could deserve, and for which no thanks are adequate, and which

I can only acknowledge. One of the greatest sins in life is to take things for granted. I said that Kate did not read my books. I hope that she will read this one, for I want her to know, and I want everyone to know, that without her life for me would be impossible.

2

SELF PORTRAIT

The first sentence of any book or of any chapter is always the most difficult to write. Get it down, and the material will flow. If that is ordinarily true, how much truer it must be of a chapter in which a writer proposes to write about himself. Juvenal, the Roman satirist, wrote: 'The maxim "Know thyself" comes down to us from the skies; it should be imprinted in the heart, and stored in the memory, whether you are looking for a wife, or wishing for a seat in the sacred senate.' Some said that 'Know thyself' was the response of the oracle at Delphi to Croesus. Some said that it was the response of Apollo to Chilon when he asked what man's highest good was. Some said that the Seven Wise Men of Greece came to Apollo's Temple to dedicate to him the first-fruits of their wisdom, and that wisdom was summed up in two sayings—'Know thyself', and, 'All things in moderation'. Cicero said that, since the saying was greater than the human mind could have envisaged, it was attributed to God. Maybe Thomas Carlyle was wise when he spoke of, 'the folly of that impossible precept "Know thyself", till it be translated into the partially possible one, "Know what thou canst work at".' If a man cannot know himself, he can at least know what he can and cannot do. But where to start—that is the question.

Paul discerns three elements in each one of us—body, mind and spirit. This will make a pattern for me.

First, then, the body. When I was talking about childhood days, I said that in the first five years after we came to Motherwell, I managed to acquire seven illnesses. For the next fifty years I did not know what illness was. I played all games and played them hard—football, cricket, golf, tennis, running—and I played them well enough to share the sports' championship of the school. So long as it was possible I kept on playing games. Collin Brooks writes in one of his books: 'We should, like children and like most birds, take every opportunity of playing', and I believe that. Physical fitness and mental fitness go hand in hand. But the day came when I had to stop. First, a bout of pneumonia and then a spell of acute bronchitis put an end to all that. The John of the Revelation looked on heaven as a place where there will be no more sea. I have come to look on heaven as a place where there will be no more stairs. But since my job requires me to talk and not to walk, work has not been too badly affected.

For many years I have been stone deaf, but a very wonderful hearing-aid has enabled me to overcome that handicap almost completely, so completely that until this year my main hobby was conducting choirs. To tell the truth, being deaf can be a positive advantage. It means that it is possible to sleep anywhere—even in a railway station. And—most useful of all—it means that you need only listen to what you want to listen to. If the speaker is boring, then it is the easiest thing in the world to switch him off! I think it was Dr Johnson who related how on one occasion someone boringly talked and talked and talked. 'What did you do?' Johnson was asked, and answered, 'I detached my thoughts and thought of Tom Thumb.' I don't need to make even that effort—I can retire into a world of my own whenever I want to.

A word on hearing-aids. Some people do not like to wear one, because it makes them noticeable. You are far more noticeable when you are deaf than when you are wearing a hearing-aid, because for some strange reason people are full of sympathy for the blind but find deaf people no better than a nuisance. 'You shall not curse the deaf,' says the Law of the Bible (Lev. 19.14). And one word of advice from one who has been deaf for forty years—a hearing-aid must not be constantly switched off and on. It is because they do that that many people never succeed in mastering their aid. It is like dentures, or glasses, or an artificial limb. If it has to be worn, it should be worn from the minute you get up in the morning until the time you go to bed at night, until it becomes an inseparable part of you. Of course, I would like not to be deaf, but I have never found that being deaf has stopped me doing anything that I wanted to do.

So much for the body—and that was easy—for about being breathless and deaf there is no argument. And now for the mind.

First and foremost, I have an essentially second-class mind. Margot Asquith tells how her husband Asquith, the Prime Minister, said to her after a dinner party that the person he had been placed next to, and had had to talk to, had 'a lending library mind'. I don't know if I would say that of myself, but I have a second-class mind. It is the simple truth that I never had an original idea in my life. In all the books I have written I have explained and expounded other men's ideas.

When Barrie was given the freedom of Dumfries, he spoke of his days as a pupil at Dumfries Academy, and he said: 'I always knew that I could get the second prize without working much, but that I could never get the first, however hard I tried.' I wasn't dux of Dalziel High. True to form, I was *proxime accessit*, runner-up. There was a girl there called Irene Tyrell. She was dux, and when she was around I was a natural second. Fortunately, she did not take Greek—and in Greek I had it all my own way. If then I have a second-class mind, how did I emerge with a first-class honours degree in Classics? Because I happen to have a phenomenal memory, and I am therefore an excellent examinee—which merely goes to show what a poor test of real ability examinations are. As near as makes no practical difference I never forget what I have read, or at least I know where to find it.

But how with a second-class mind did I write all my books and end up teaching in a university? There is more than one reason.

First, an honours degree in Classics has always been the blue ribband of a university career. At first sight to spend one's academic training acquiring a specialised knowledge of 'dead' languages seems a profitless enterprise. But Dorothy Sayers once wrote:

> The tools of learning are the same in any and every subject; and the person who knows how to use them will, at any age, get the mastery of a new subject in half the time and with a quarter of the effort expended by the person who had not the tools at his command.

I am firmly convinced to this day that the mental discipline of the Classics is the best preparation for any other form of study. I had the inestimable advantage of beginning with a trained mind.

Second, I can and do work. Collin Brooks said: 'The art of writing is the art of applying the seat of the pants to the seat of the chair.' This I can do—and in this I am in good company. Balzac spoke of himself as 'plying the pick for dear life like an entombed miner'. Flaubert spoke of himself as 'sick, irritated, the prey a thousand times a day of cruel pain', but, 'continuing my labour like a true workingman, who, with sleeves turned up, in the sweat of his brow, beats away at his anvil, whether it rain or blow, hail or thunder'. Beverley Nicholas tells of a talk he had with Winston Churchill. Nichols had just written *Prelude*, and had at one stroke achieved fame. Churchill asked him how long he had taken to write it. Nichols said that it had been written in spasms over five months, Churchill demanded if Nichols did not go to his desk every morning and write. Beverley Nichols said he had to wait for the mood and the inspiration. 'Nonsense!' Churchill answered. 'You should go to your room every morning at nine o'clock, and say, "I'm going to write for four hours".' Nichols asked what about toothache, indigestion, the inability to get down to it. Churchill answered: 'You've got to get over that. If you sit waiting for inspiration, you will sit waiting until you are an old man. Writing is like any other job—like marching an army, for instance. If you sit down and wait until the weather is fine, you won't get far with your troops. Kick yourself; irritate yourself; but *write*; it's the only way.' The most extraordinary example of all is that of W. B. Yeats who tells how he owed everything to Lady Gregory who every morning at 11 a.m. shut him into his study to write a poem! Lyrics to order—yes, and lyrics which the memory of men will never willingly let die.

I understand this thoroughly. When I was a parish minister, I never wrote a sermon after Thursday. The great peril of the parish ministry is that a man is his own master. He can waste his mornings; he can put off writing while he waits for inspiration. Some men break down—and little wonder, for Saturday night finds them first desperately searching for a text and then still more desperately writing. How can an exhausted man preach on Sunday morning? There is no reason for this if two conditions are fulfilled—

one, that a man preaches systematically and the other that he exercises a teaching ministry. Nothing has done more harm to the pulpit than 'topical' preaching. If a man is constantly seeking ideas out of his own head, he will certainly be in trouble. If he pronounces on this, that and the next thing, he will be talking about things about which he knows nothing. He is the trained expert in only one sphere—the Bible and the Christian faith. There is no reason why he should not sit down at any time and in a sermon expound a doctrine, go through the Apostles' Creed, take a parable and write on it, preach his way through a book of the Bible. Of course, every sermon will end with the practical impact of all this. But no man need sit and wait for inspiration, no man need be feverishly toiling at the last minute, if he will use his God-given tools with the expertise he has been taught.

I know I have a second-class mind, but I can sit down and work. I don't make the slightest claim to inspiration in preaching or writing. I only claim to have gone to work as any working man must go.

Third, I can work to order. Just because I have nothing original to say, I can accept a commission to say something which some one else wants to be said. When Haydn was asked why he had never written a piano quintette, his answer was: 'Because no one ever commissioned one', or, as we might put it more crudely: 'No one ever ordered one.' When Bach was organist of St Thomas's Church, Leipzig, he was pouring out his immortal music to be sung as anthems by the church choir Sunday by Sunday. It was being done as a job, as a professional day-to-day undertaking. I suppose that I must have written more than fifty books, and the plain fact is that I never chose to write one single one of them. Some one would come to me and say: 'Will you do a Bible Class Handbook on such and such a subject?' and I would undertake to do it. That is even the case with this the most personal book I have ever written. It is written because I was asked to write it.

I suppose that the outstanding example of this was the way in which the Daily Study Bible was written. More than a million copies of it have been sold. It all began in this way. The Church of Scotland was using a series of daily bible readings prepared by an association famous for such readings. Through no fault of the association or of the writers this series did not sell, and the association involved was forced to discontinue them. The then Publications Manager of the Church of Scotland came to me and said very bluntly: 'Would you be prepared to do us a volume of daily bible readings as a stopgap until we get some one decent to do them for us?' I immediately agreed. When the first volume was coming to an end they still had not got 'some one decent'. So I did a second, and so on and on until the whole New Testament had been covered.

I have always been perfectly willing to write to order, and I have never seen anything in the least insulting in being asked to do so. I knew that I could say nothing new; but I also knew that I had a certain gift for taking what far greater scholars than I had said and putting it into a form in which people with no technical education could read it. A. S. Peake claimed that he was 'a theological middleman', and that is the only claim I can make. I knew that I could read quickly and that I could assimilate what others had said. I knew that I could 'pre-digest' it and put it into an easily understandable form. And I knew that I could do it in time, even if it meant sometimes delivering the copy to the printer at three o'clock in the morning.

Just because I have such a very ordinary mind, and just because I am not troubled with original ideas struggling to be expressed, I could work, and I could work to order, and make available for others the work of men far greater than myself. I could at least be the pipe-line which brought the living springs to others, even if I had not drunk at these springs myself. Bertram Pollock, a former Bishop of Lincoln, said in his autobiography that the problem of preaching was to speak *non nova sed nove*, not fresh things but in a fresh way. I may be only indulging in self-defence and self-justification, but I think that there is something to be said for the conviction that it is important to make the old truths live with a new life, to compel men to see the true meaning of that which they have always known, to stab them awake to the wonder of the great things which they have dully accepted. Discovery is important—but so is rediscovery.

Fourth, this has been made easier for me because of the fact that I have never had any difficulty in self-expression either in speaking or in writing. I have always been able to make words do what I want them to do. I have always hated jargon. I have always asked myself and other people one ever-recurring question: 'What do you mean by that?' John Wesley tells us how in his young days he took his sermons and read them to an old domestic servant, telling her to stop him every time he said something that she did not understand. His manuscripts became masses of changes and alterations and rubbings out and additions—but they were intelligible. Wesley wrote:

> I design plain truth for plain people; therefore, of set purpose I abstain from all nice and philosophical speculations; from all perplexed and intimate reasonings; and, as far as possible, from even the show of learning. I labour to avoid all words which are not easy to understand, all which are not used in common life; and, in particular, those kinds of technical terms that so frequently occur in Bodies of Divinity; those modes of speaking which men of reading are intimately acquainted with, but which to the common people are an unknown tongue.

It has been my good fortune to have been able to use words in a way that non-technical people could understand, and it has been my deliberate practice to keep on asking myself and everyone else: 'What do you mean by that?' And, if I could attach no definite meaning to any statement, then that statement, however impressive it sounded, had to go.

Fifth, this was made easier for me because of the fact that I am no theologian. I know Greek and know it intimately. I know a great deal about the life and the thought of the world into which Jesus came. I know what the New Testament says, and I can at least to some extent explain it to others. But I cannot think in abstractions at all; I think in pictures. The professional theologians leave me faint—and not even pursuing, and sometimes I am tempted to agree with the cynical verdict that they write books which no one but another theologian can read, and that they produce confusion and call it theology. Because I need simple things myself, I can talk simply to others—and I am well aware that there are times when, with me, simplification becomes over-simplification.

What I have done I have done with a second-class mind, an ability to toil and to toil to order, with some gift of words and some ability to communicate, even at the expense, sometimes at least, of over-simplification.

And so to the last part of the human make-up—the spirit.

First and foremost, I was born without a temper. I can be irritated and annoyed, but I do not ever remember being really angry, and I have never quarrelled with anyone in my life. This is by no means altogether a good thing. Darwin said of Graham, the editor: 'He was perhaps not easily enough disturbed.' I tend to run away from things, and to avoid all unpleasantness. Margot Asquith said of her husband the Prime Minister: 'He never put to sea in a storm.' And that is true of me. I have often in my life failed to administer the rebuke I ought to have administered, failed to intervene in the situation in which I ought to have intervened, for no better reason than that I shrank from trouble. Closely allied with this is a habit of putting off the thing I do not want to do simply because I do not want to face it, and the result is that it is often too late to face the thing at all.

Sir Hector Hetherington was one of the great university Principals. Few men could handle a difficult team in the way in which he could handle it. On one occasion one of his more belligerent members of staff, convinced that he had a legitimate grievance which was not getting the attention it deserved, sent to the Principal an extremely angry letter, replete with complaints and threats in equal proportions. The Principal duly received the letter. A day or two afterwards he met the sender. He met him with no ill-will at all. 'James,' he said (James was not in fact his name—no names, no pack-drill), 'that was a wonderful letter you wrote to me—*but why did you post it*?' I might have wanted to write the letter; but all the likelihood is that I would have put it off until it was too late to write it, and far too late to post it. My lack of temper is not due to discipline, still less to Christian forbearance; it is due to fear of unpleasantness, which often makes me put up with something rather than take any action about it.

Second, I am quite sure that belief is easier for some people than for others. Some people are what you might call natural believers, and some people are what you might call natural doubters. I am very much a natural believer. It is not that life has been specially easy for me. I shall later on talk of the blows that life has launched against me; but I have never found myself doubting God and the love of God.

It is not that I do not like argument. I love the cut and thrust of debate. It is not that I have all the problems neatly solved and filed away. There seem to be two different and even contradictory sides to me. One half of me will doubt everyone and everything; but somehow there is something deeper. The debates and the doubts are thrilling mental gymnastics; they give me what Beatrice Webb called the stimulus of the mental hike; and I love the mental wrestling of debate. I feel like James Agate, the great dramatic critic, when he said: 'I don't know very much, but what I do know, I know better than anybody, and I don't want to argue about it . . . My mind is not a bed to be made and remade.' And so often I will argue just for the joy of arguing, and I will say the most outrageous things just to provoke the person I am arguing with. But in the deepest part of me there is a certainty which nothing can touch, and later I will talk about the things most surely believed.

Third, there are few, very few, people with whom I am really friends. I have crowds of acquaintances, many people whose company I enjoy, but there are very few with whom I am really intimate. I think that I would seem to be a friendly, open person, but there are very few people with whom I am on first name terms, and I am a little shocked at the modern habit of indiscriminately greeting people with a kiss when they meet us.

Because I was a parish minister for years, and have been a teacher for still more years, many people have at one time or another opened their hearts to me—and I do not think that I ever revealed anyone's secret to anyone else. People used to say to my wife: 'He'll have told you such and such a thing,' only to find that I had not mentioned it even to her. But I wonder if there is anyone to whom I would open my own heart. Margot Asquith said that she could never talk to Balfour about religion. 'He had,' she said, 'a little private property in his mind, in which was written at the portal, "Trespassers forbidden".' I think that I am rather like that. There was an older minister for whom I had a very great respect and affection; he was a mystic and a saint and a very great soul. But he talked a great deal about his own faults and self-revilings, and he expected others to be as open. You would go and see him, and he would say: 'I'm so glad to see you; I've been wanting a talk with you. Come and slap your soul on the table and let's open our hearts to each other.' And it always made me slightly sick so that instead of talking I would clam up in silence. All this is perhaps mixed up with the fact that I dislike being touched, except by a very few people. In some ways I am a very gregarious person, what Dr Johnson called a clubbable man, but somehow I like to keep my distance, and I like a decent reticence.

Fourth, I am a very tolerant person, and the older I get the more tolerant I become. I have always felt that, especially in a teacher, it is an almost essential quality that one should never be shocked. T. R. Glover quotes a Cambridge saying: 'Whatsoever thy hand findeth to do, remember that other people think differently.' I am sure that George Russell was right when he said: 'There are as many ways of climbing to the stars as there are people to climb.' I am not likely to condemn a man's beliefs. If through them he has found his way to God, then that is his affair. I shall only think him wrong, if he refuses to extend to me the same sympathy that I extend to him. The one attitude that I believe to be wrong is the attitude of the man who believes that he has a monopoly of the truth and that there is no way to God but his way. Still less would I condemn a man's actions, for I am old enough to have learned to say: 'There but for the grace of God go I.'

Fifth, in more than one sense I am a worldly person. In a very real sense I love the world and all that is in it. That is why I have always been opposed to seminary teaching for the man who intends to become a minister of the Church. He is far better to do his training in the Divinity Faculty of a university, where he will be brought into contact with all kinds of subjects and all kinds of people. That great scholar and mystic von Hügel once wrote to a lady who objected to turning to Homer and Pindar from Tertullian and Augustine:

> If there is one danger for religion, if there is any one plausible, all but irresistible trend, which throughout its long rich history has sapped its force and prepared the most destructive counter excesses, it is just that—that allowing of the fascination of grace to deaden and ignore the beauties and the duties of nature.

Tertullian spoke of how he could not see a rose, or the feather from a bird's wing without thinking of God. This is why I am sure that the man who reads nothing but theology and 'religious' books will do himself and his message an infinite deal of harm. This is why a man should have as many friends and contacts as possible outside the narrow circle of the Church and the ministry. All my life I have found many of my most valuable friendships with the scientists and the medicals and the people who have no university background at all. I take no delight in saying so—I am ashamed to say so—there is in me a strain of anti-clericalism. I have hardly ever been a member of a church committee. I have neglected attendance at presbytery; and since the Presbytery of Glasgow very rightly declares that its members cannot be members of General Assembly unless they have put in five attendances at presbytery in the course of the year, I have not been a member of General Assembly for over twenty years. In all this it is I who am the loser, but I have often found myself closer to those whose work is in the world than to those whose work is in the Church.

Since I am trying to be honest I must confess that I am worldly in the sense that I like my comforts. I would rather have a week's holiday in real comfort than a month in more primitive conditions. When I was on the road doing a lot of travelling to lecture and to preach, I would never accept private hospitality, because I have always felt the need and even the necessity of being able to shut the door and be by myself. I have always liked the Jewish saying that a man will give account for every good thing he might have enjoyed and did not. I have always wanted to be involved in the world and not to withdraw from it, and I have always looked on life as something to be enjoyed.

Sixth, still to continue in the confessional, I am fundamentally a lazy person. Jerome K. Jerome said that he loved work—he could sit and look at it all day! To say that I am lazy seems to contradict what I have already said about work, and it seems to be contradicted by the number of books which I have written. What I mean is that I have constantly to struggle against a feeling of inertia. Once I get started it is all right; it is the getting started. So I have found that the only way to overcome this inertia is to commit myself to delivering something on a certain date— and then it just has to be done. Unless I had a delivery date, I don't think I would ever begin anything, let alone finish it.

Lastly, I have been teaching in this university since 1947, and I have to ask, what have I been like as a teacher? I want to set down two quotations. The first is from H. A. L. Fisher's *An Unfinished Autobiography*. Fisher tells how F. W. Maitland once said to him:

> No one should teach philosophy at a university, unless he either thinks he has it in him to make a system of his own, or is zealous to preach the system of another.

That is to say, Maitland believed that a man should teach in order to make converts to his way of thinking, and this would be true not only of philosophy but of any subject which can be taught from a stance. The second is from Somerset Maugham's autobiography, *Summing up*:

I do not seek to persuade anyone. I am devoid of the pedagogic instinct, and when I know a thing never feel in myself the desire to impart it to others. I do not much care if people agree with me. Of course, I think I am right, otherwise I should not think as I do, and they are wrong, but it does not offend me that they should be wrong.

I find myself much nearer Somerset Maugham than to F. W. Maitland. In teaching my first desire has always been to interest the listener; if I don't interest him, he will soon stop being a listener. But I have never been eager that he should think as I think, but only that he should think. I hope that he will agree with me, but, if he does not, I shall be well content if he will examine his own beliefs in the light of what I say. The only kind of person who really 'offends' me, to use Somerset Maugham's word, is the person with the shut mind who refuses even to think about what is said to him, the person who deliberately misunderstands, the person who substitutes parrot cries for thought, and, worst of all, the person who criticises a writer without ever having read a word of his books. I hope that I have always taught in order to stimulate and to awaken, and never to indoctrinate and stifle. I can honestly say that that there are few things which delight me more than to find a student in an essay or examination making a reasoned case *against* what I have taught him. It is good teaching if a man can be induced to examine his beliefs and to question them and even to change them; it is good teaching if a man has to put new things through his mind and emerges with his own beliefs still more firmly based. The only bad teaching is the teaching which leaves the listener completely uninterested, completely indifferent, unmoved to learn and unstimulated to think.

Such then is my portrait of myself, and, even if it is all delusion, it will make it easier to understand why I believe what I believe.

3

I BELIEVE

Sooner or later this chapter has to be written. A man must decide the things by which he lives. It is true that there is everything to be said for the open mind, but there is nothing to be said for the mind which is open at both ends. Lord Balfour, the once famous Prime Minister, said: 'Nothing matters very much, and very few things matter at all.' That is the remark of a weary cynic. It is true that very few things matter, but these few things matter intensely. It is possible to overdo the 'reverent agnosticism'. Life cannot always be lived in an enchanted mist. Uncertainty means the paralysis of action; belief and action go hand in hand. Bishop Creighton said: 'The one real object of education is to leave a man in the condition of continually asking questions.' That is true, but G. K. Chesterton said with equal truth that we have asked all the questions that there are to ask, and that it is time we stopped asking questions and started looking for answers. It is quite true that, as some one has said, a teacher should be an 'animated question mark'. But asking the right questions must clearly be the first stage on the road to finding at least some of the right answers, and the teacher must also be a signpost in the right directions.

I have already said that I am a simple-minded person. I have neither a philosophical nor a theological mind. For that reason I need to think in pictures. As Régine Pernoud says in her book *Heloise and Abelard*:

> There is a world of difference between learning to repeat 'God is an omnipotent being' and learning to address oneself straight to God saying: 'Thou art my rock'.

But granted that I must think in that way, I still must think. The New Testament is clear about the importance of a man coming to his own conclusions. There was a day when Jesus asked his disciples: 'Who do men say that the Son of Man is?' And when they had told him what others were saying and the opinions to which others had come, he demanded: 'But *you*—who do *you* say that I am?' (Matt. 16.14,15). As John tells the story, when Pilate asked Jesus: 'Are you the King of the Jews?' Jesus said to him: 'Do you say this of your own accord, or did others say it to you about me?' (John 18.34), Is this your own discovery, or is it only a carried story which you have heard from someone else? 'Test everything,' said Paul, 'hold fast that which is good' (1 Thess. 5.21). As Robert Frost has written: 'The best way out is always through.' The obligation of thought, the obligation of thinking out his own faith is laid on every Christian. James Douglas has said bitterly: 'Education is a state-controlled manufactory of echoes.' No teacher would wish to get back from his students a mere echo of what he has said to them. Epictetus said with a certain vivid crudity that sheep do not vomit up the grass to show the shepherd how much they have eaten. They turn it into wool and milk. The aim of teaching is not to produce an echo, but to enable a man to think his way to an independent faith.

To think then is a necessity of the Christian life. T. R. Glover, in his book *The World of the New Testament*, closes his chapter on the Greek by saying that it was the Greek point of view:

Everything must be examined; . . . there is no question which it is wrong for man to ask; Nature in the long run must stand and deliver; God too must explain himself, for did he not make man so?

Clive Bell writes:

Only reason can convince us of these three fundamental truths without a recognition of which there can be no effective liberty; that what we believe is not necessarily true; that what we like is not necessarily good; and that all questions are open.

Ambrose Bierce in *The Devil's Dictionary* defined faith: 'Faith: noun: Belief without evidence in what is told by one who speaks without knowledge of things without parallel.' This is not very far from Tertullian's 'I believe because it is impossible'.

The Christian point of view is not unintelligent acceptance, nor is it total dependence on human reason. The Christian point of view was long ago perfectly summed up by Anselm: 'I do not seek to understand so that I may believe; rather do I believe that I may understand.' The Christian does not begin with what the human intellect has discovered. The Christian begins with what God has revealed. Faith is founded on revealed truth. First, the Christian accepts that which God has revealed; in that revelation he believes by faith. And then, and then only, he applies his reason to it, that faith may be a rational understanding of that which has been believed. The Christian mind, the Christian reason does not operate within a vacuum; it operates within the sphere which revelation has provided and upon the material which has not been humanly discovered, but which has been given by God. To put this in another way, Christian thought and Christian experience will go hand in hand. As Anselm had it:

He who has not believed will not experience, and he who has not experienced will not understand; for just as experiencing a thing is better than hearing about it, so knowledge that stems from experience outweighs knowledge derived through hearsay.

So then it is not: 'I think and I believe'; it is: 'I believe and I think.' It is this combination of divine revelation and human reason which produces the real certainty. Xenophon tells how Socrates said to the young man: 'How do you know that? Do you know it? Or, are you guessing?' 'I am guessing,' said the young man. 'Very well,' said Socrates, 'when we are done with guessing, and when we know, shall we talk about it then?' Guessing turns to certainty when the mind of man and the Spirit of God meet.

In matters of belief there is only one way to begin—I believe in God. I said that I was simple-minded and the old Paley argument still appeals to me. Suppose a man is crossing a moor and suppose in the middle of the moor he comes upon a watch lying on the ground. Suppose this man has never in his life seen a watch before and does not know what a watch is or what it is for. What will happen? He picks it up and examines it. He finds that it is composed of a metal case and a porcelain dial. He opens it. Inside he finds a complicated arrangement of springs and cogged wheels and levers and jewels, all ticking away. He looks at the hands on the dial and he quickly sees that they are moving in a predetermined order. What does he say? Does he say: 'I suppose that all these things, the metal, the springs, the lever, the jewels, the porcelain by chance came together from the ends of the earth, by chance made themselves into all these various parts, by chance wound themselves up, by chance made themselves into a watch and set themselves going'? No. If he has any powers of reasoning at all, he will be bound to say: 'I have found a watch.

Somewhere there must be a watch-maker.' So when we find a universe which has an order more accurate than any watch, it is natural to say: 'Somewhere there must be a world-maker.' Order implies mind; there must be a mind in it and behind it all. An orrery is a working model of the solar system. If we go into an exhibition where there is an orrery on show, we know immediately that some one designed and built that orrery; it could not have come into existence without a mind to plan it and a hand to build it. If this is so of the model, must it not be just as true of the reality of which the orrery is a model? May we not say that beyond and behind the system of the universe there is a mind and a maker?

Further, within the universe itself we see a process of evolution in which man has come to be what he is after millions and millions of years of development. The long climb from the amoeba to the man—may we not see design and purpose there? According to at least one view of modern science that is precisely what we cannot see. Jacques Monod wrote in his famous book *Chance and Necessity*, which was translated into English in 1972, that under the microscope, from bacteria to man, there is a 'chemical machinery' which in all cases is the same, and which is unvarying and invariable. The system is locked into itself, unaffected by anything from outside. 'The cell is a *machine*.' If that was all that there was to it, there never could be any change in any direction. There could not be consciousness or life or any other living thing. What then is responsible for the advance that is in evolution? The answer is mutations. And what is the character of these mutations? They are completely unpredictable, completely unforeseeable, the product of pure chance. As R. C. Zaehner, describing this process of chance, writes:

Life, and consciousness, and man are dependent on pure chance, what Monod calls 'essential' chance. Man, then, so far from being the result and end product of some immanent will or vital principle working within Nature is quite literally a freak produced by pure chance operating on a microscopic machine which nevertheless determines his whole development. Man is finally dethroned and made the plaything of a mindless universe.

Monod claims that for modern biology the sole conceivable hypothesis is that 'chance alone is at the source of every innovation. Pure chance, absolutely free but blind, is at the very root of the stupendous edifice of evolution.'

In principle it is all very like the conclusion arrived at by Epicurus two thousand years ago and more. Epicurus said that in the beginning there was nothing but atoms falling through the void. They fell in straight lines like rain and to the end of time there would have been nothing but atoms falling through the void but for one thing—the atoms were somehow or other endowed with the power to swerve. When they swerved they knocked into each other and made clusters. If they rebounded widely, the result was gases; if they rebounded less widely, the result was liquids; if they rebounded very closely the result was solids. And so man and everything else in the world are no more than 'fortuitous conglomerations of atoms'.

So in the ancient days and still now everything is reduced to chance. There are scientists who find this very difficult to accept. Back in 1954 Albert Einstein said: 'I cannot believe that God plays dice with the cosmos.' Can we really accept the hypothesis of all-pervading, all-dominating chance? We look at the universe and the characteristic of the universe is order. Does chance really produce order? Is chance not in its very nature an erratic and haphazard force? We look at the evolution of man. If it is all a matter of chance, why is there this steady process upwards? The more we look at the world and at man, the more we feel that chance appears to be only another name for purpose, because if chance is the moving force, then chance has achieved what mind and purpose would have achieved. I think that it is more difficult to believe in a chance which can produce order than in a mind which did produce it.

I realise quite clearly that in these matters I am a child, and that anything I say may be, to a scientist, no more than a matter for amusement, but ever since I knew anything about the evolutionary process an idea has been in my mind. Evolution has never happened on a broad front with living creatures advancing like a united army. Evolution has always happened—it would seem—not like one great advancing line, but rather in the shape of a wedge with some one creature out in front, with bit by bit more creatures following this creature. So some living organism was the first to come out of the water on to the dry land. Some living organism was the first to stand upright. Some living organism was the first to learn to use tools, to think and to plan, to look before and after, to remember the past and to plan for the future. This has always seemed to me to mean that at each stage some one living creature responded to some kind of stimulation, while the others did not. The one which responded became the means to the next step forward. The ones which refused to respond were either eliminated, because they became so adapted to their environment that when the environment changed they could not continue to exist; or, they continued on lesser lines, having missed the highest. If this is true, then the progress of evolution has been due, not to chance, but to invitation and response. And that bears with it the staggering thought that every single living thing in the world, even every blade of grass, might have been a man, if somewhere back along the line the response to invitation had been made. It may well be that any such ideas will produce only amused contempt for my ignorance, but I find a theory of

A SPIRITUAL AUTOBIOGRAPHY

invitation and response at least as easy for the mind to believe in as a theory of pure chance.

Because I believe in God in this way, I believe in the world. The first dangerous heretics with whom the Church had to deal were the Gnostics. The Gnostics faced the age-old problem of sin and suffering, and asked how a good God could have made a world where there are things like that. The explanation they produced was this. They said that from the beginning there were two entities, spirit and matter. Matter was not created; it was always there. Spirit is altogether good; but from the beginning matter was flawed and evil; it did not *become* evil, it *is* essentially evil. Out of this flawed matter the world was made. God being pure spirit could not himself touch this flawed matter, for the perfect cannot touch the evil. So then God sent out a series of aeons or emanations, each one a little more distant from himself. The further away from God the aeons became, the more ignorant of God they became. At last in the series a point is reached at which the aeons are not only ignorant of God; they are hostile to God. So the series arrives at an aeon, who is ignorant of God, distant from God, and hostile to God; and by this aeon the world was made. The world, therefore, as the Gnostics saw it, was made out of bad stuff by an ignorant and inferior God who was hostile to the true God. All material things are therefore evil. The world is evil; the body is evil. The world is to be hated and the body is to be continually suspected and despised. It is a view which the Church condemned, but from which the Church never wholly escaped, for in our own life-time the Church has gloomily sung that 'Earth is a desert drear', and has regarded sex as something dirty and something of which to be ashamed.

Marcion was the man who towards the end of the second century preached the Gnostic doctine, and Tertullian was the man who opposed him. Even the Greek Plutarch could

insist that Nature loved beauty and had made the peacock
for the sake of the iridescent colours of its tail. Tertullian
wrote in the same way, as T. R. Glover translates him: 'One
flower of the hedgerow by itself, I think—I do not say a
flower from the meadows: one shell of any sea you like—
I do not say the Red Sea; one feather of a moor-fowl—to
say nothing of a peacock—will they speak to you of a
mean Creator?' 'If I offer you a rose, you will not scorn its
Creator.' Jesus felt the same way about the beauty of God's
world. 'Consider the lilies of the field, how they grow;
they neither toil nor spin; yet I tell you, even Solomon in
all his glory was not arrayed like one of these' (Matt.
6.28,29). To look at the world is to see God. As Joseph Mary
Plunkett wrote:

> I see his blood upon the rose
> And in the stars the glory of his eyes,
> His body gleams amid eternal snows,
> His tears fall from the skies.
>
> I see his face in every flower;
> The thunder and the singing of the birds
> Are but his voice—and carven by his power
> Rocks are his written words.
>
> All pathways by his feet are worn,
> His strong heart stirs the ever-beating sea,
> His crown of thorns is twined with every thorn,
> His cross is every tree.

I believe in God—and I believe in God the Creator—and I
believe in the loveliness of the world.

Because I believe in God like this, I believe that God
should be the daily companion of the common way and
not only the refuge in emergency. For many God only
begins to be thought of when everything else has failed. God

is the last refuge when everything else is gone. So Shakespeare describes the dying of Falstaff:

> So a' cried out God, God! three or four times. Now I, to comfort him, bid him a' should not think of God, I hoped there was no need to trouble himself with any such thoughts yet.

There is a conversation in Brecht's *Mother Courage*. The chaplain says to Mother Courage: 'We're in God's hands now!' And her answer is: 'I hope we're not as desperate as that, but it *is* hard to sleep at night.' Clarence Day in *Life with Father* gives an almost grotesque instance of how his father reacted to God like that: 'Apparently now that he was in trouble, his thoughts had turned to God. "Have mercy!" they heard him shouting indignantly. "I say have mercy, damn it!"'

I do not say that we can always feel the need and the presence of God with the same intensity, but I do say that true religion means never altogether forgetting the presence of God.

Because I believe in God like this, I believe in the love of God. I do not believe that God's love is a sloppy and sentimental attitude to us. Seneca, the great Stoic, said of God *fortiter amat*, he loves us gallantly, courageously; he loves us with a love which is also strength. There will therefore be times when the way will be hard, so that the muscle of the soul will be developed. There will be times when I have to learn that I cannot go my way and escape the consequences, for love and discipline so far from being antithetic are complementary. It has always to be remembered that the Greek word which in the New Testament is translated *to tempt* can equally mean *to test*. The *temptations* of Jesus were the *testing* of Jesus. In the older translations the Abraham-Isaac story begins with the statement that God *tempted* Abraham (Gen. 22.1). Clearly, it is impossible to think of God taking steps to seduce Abraham into sin. God *tested* Abraham. Temptation is not meant to make us fall; it is meant to confront us with a situation out of which we emerge stronger than we were. Temptation is not the penalty of manhood; it is the glory of manhood.

Because I believe this, I believe that pain and suffering are never the will of God for his children. I was never able, in the days when I was a pastor of people, to go into a house where some one was stricken with illness—perhaps cancer, perhaps a condition which would leave life a living death—and say: 'This is the will of God.' I could never go into a family where there had been death by accident or where a young person had died too soon and say: 'This is the will of God.' I cannot conceive that it is the will of God that anyone should be run over by a driver under the influence of drink, or that a young mother should die of leukaemia, or that some one in the first flush of youth should face the increasing helplessness of arterio-sclerosis. When these things happen, I am quite certain that there is no one sorrier than God. In *The Devil's Dictionary* Ambrose Bierce thus defines Patience: 'a noun: a minor form of despair disguised as a virtue.' When things like that happen, we are not meant to accept them with folded hands; we are meant to do all that we can to see that we do not allow them to happen again. Jesus said: 'If it is by the finger of God I cast out demons, then the kingdom of God has come upon you' (Luke 11.20). The coming of the kingdom involves the defeat of disease and pain.

I knew a woman whose daughter was killed by an electrical household accident, electrocuted by an electric blanket. There was a fatal accident enquiry, and the verdict was that it was 'an act of God'. The mother was shattered. Of course, it is only a legal formula to denote something of which the explanation is undiscoverable, but there are few more blasphemous phrases in the English language. At that time there was no one sorrier than God that something which should never have happened had happend to one of his children.

I had in my own experience a wounding attribution of events to the will of God. The BBC asked me to do a week's 'ten to eight' in the morning talks on radio, and they asked me to take as a subject the modern approach to the miracles of Jesus. It was not a subject which I myself would have chosen, but I agreed to do it. The line I took was a line that I have always taken. I have always felt that Jesus is to be regarded, not as a person who *did* things nineteen hundred years ago, but as a person who *does* things now. I therefore said that the miracles were often not so much stories of what Jesus once did, but symbols of what he still can do. I spoke of the stilling of the storm, and I said that if Jesus did still a storm on the Lake of Galilee in AD 28, it meant very little to me. But it is different if the lesson of the story is that in any storm of life there is in the presence of Jesus confidence and calm, that the storms Jesus stills are in the hearts of men, so that, no matter what tempest of trouble or pain or sorrow may blow upon life, with him there is calm. On the last day of the week instead of a talk I was interviewed by David Winter. He asked me how I had come to this way of looking at things. I told him the truth. I told him that some years ago our twenty-one year old daughter and the lad to whom she would some day have been married were both drowned in a yachting accident. I said that God did not stop that accident at sea, but he did still the storm in my own heart, so that somehow my wife and I came through that terrible time still on our own two feet. The letters after the broadcasts began to come in, and there came an anonymous letter from Northern Ireland: 'Dear Dr Barclay, I know now why God killed your daughter; it was to save her from being corrupted by your heresies.' *I know now why God killed your daughter.* That—

the accidental destruction of the beautiful and the good—
the will of God. If I had had that writer's address, I would
have written back, not in anger—the inevitable blaze of
anger was over in a flash—but in pity, and I would have
said to him, as John Wesley said to someone: 'Your God is
my devil.' The day my daughter was lost at sea there was
sorrow in the heart of God.

When things like that happen, there are just three things
to be said. First, to understand them is impossible. Second,
Jesus does not offer us solutions to them. What he does offer
us is his strength and help somehow to accept what we
cannot understand. Third, the one fatal reaction is the
bitter resentment which for ever after meets life with a
chip on the shoulder and a grudge against God. The one
saving reaction is simply to go on living, to go on working,
and to find in the presence of Jesus Christ the strength and
courage to meet life with steady eyes, and to know the
comfort that God too is afflicted in my affliction.

Because I believe in God and in the love of God, I
believe in prayer. But over the years of life I have learned
certain things about prayer, things which it is essential to
remember. I think that there are a great many people who
do not pray because they have come to the concluson that
prayer just does not 'work', and that therefore there is no
point in prayer.

First, I believe that God will not do for me what I can do
for myself. Prayer must never be regarded as a labour-
saving device. If I am ill, if there is something wrong with
my body, I need not pray for cure, unless I am prepared to
take my trouble to the physician, unless I am prepared to
sacrifice certain habits and pleasures, unless I am prepared to
accept a certain discipline in my life. But if I do patiently and
strictly and obediently carry out the regimen that is prescribed for me, then I can pray, and the prayer will put me into
a condition in which the treatment will be doubly effective.

Second, I do not think that it is right to pray for things. The one thing to be said about this is that it is an acid test of a thing if you can talk about it and mention it and think about it in the presence of God at all. But I cannot think that it is right to pray for a new house or a new car or a new typewriter or even a new job. I may pray to make the best possible use of what I have, and to do the best possible work where I am; but it is not the part of prayer to ask for material things. Jesus refused to use his power to turn the stones into bread.

Third—and this I think is the most important lesson that the years have taught me—I do not think that prayer is ever evasion, that prayer saves us from having to face things which we do not want to face, and which are going to hurt if we face them. Jesus in Gethsemane discovered that there was no evasion of the Cross. Paul discovered that there was no way to be rid of that agonizing thorn in the flesh. What prayer does is to enable us, not to find a way round the hard thing, but to go straight through it, not to avoid it but to accept it and overcome it. Prayer is not evasion; prayer is conquest. Prayer does not offer me a way of escape; it offers me a way to victory. Jesus did not evade the Cross; he went through the Cross to the Resurrection. Paul did not evade the thorn; he found the all-sufficient grace, the strength of God made perfect in his weakness, the way to be more than conqueror, thorn or no thorn. So I must not pray: 'Lord, take this from me.' I must pray: 'Lord, help me to face this thing and to conquer it, and even out of the tragedy to find the glory.'

Fourth, I believe that real prayer is simply being in the presence of God. When I am in trouble, and when I go to my friend, I don't want anything from him except himself, I just want to be with him for a time, to feel his comradeship, his concern, his caring round me and about me, and then to go out to a world warmer because I spent an hour with him.

47

It must be that way with me and God. I must go to him simply for himself. And that is why I believe in intercessory prayer. I don't know the rationale of intercessory prayer. I know that God knows far better than I do what my loved ones need. I know that he does not need to be reminded of their need. But I also know what it has meant to me in the hard times of life to know that there were those who were remembering me before God. I don't know how prayer works—but then I don't know how electricity works either. I do not need to know how a thing works in order to use it and to depend upon it.

I believe in Jesus. For me Jesus is the centre and the soul of the whole matter. What do I believe about Jesus? For me the most important single text in the Bible is John 1.14: 'And the Word became flesh and dwelt among us.' What does that saying mean, and why has it, at least for me, this unique importance? In Greek the word translated *Word* is *logos*. In Greek the word *logos* has two meanings, and there is no one English word which will include both. Because of this Moffatt in his translation did not translate *logos* at all; he transliterated it. 'So the Logos became flesh and tarried among us.' Moffatt felt that, since no word could completely translate *logos*, it was better not to translate it, but to leave it to the expositor to expound the meaning.

The first meaning of *logos* is *word*. What is a word? A word is *a means of communication*. Therefore Jesus is God's means of communication to men. Again, a word is *the expression of a thought*. I think, and to express my thought to others I have to find a word. Therefore, Jesus is the expression of the thought of God. So John says: 'If you want to know what God is trying to tell us, look at Jesus. If you want to know what God is thinking, look at Jesus.' The second meaning of *logos* is *mind* or *reason*. But *logos* can mean more, much more, than simply the mind and the reason of the individual man. Long before John wrote the Fourth Gospel, six centuries before, there was a man in Ephesus called Heraclitus. He was one of the greatest of the Greek philosophers. He had two favourite sayings. First, 'Everything is in a state of flux.' The illustration he used was that, as he said, you can't step into the same river twice. Step in; step out; step in again; but the water has flowed on and it is a different river. So in life everything is in a state of flux. But there is in life another law. Always the same effect follows the same cause. If you plant turnip seeds, you will get turnips, not parsnips. This is therefore a dependable and reliable universe in which things make sense. Why? Because—and here is the second great principle of the universe—'everything happens in accordance with the *logos*'. And what is the *logos*? The *logos* is the mind of God, interpenetrating the universe and making sense of it. *The logos is the mind of God.* The Stoics developed this idea. What solves the traffic problem of the heavens? Why do the planets keep their courses and not bump into each other? What brings back day and night, summer and winter in their unvarying order? Why is H_2O always water? In other words, what makes the universe a cosmos and not a chaos? The answer is the Logos, the mind of God. It is the Logos, the mind of God, which puts order into the universe and reason into the mind of man. So John says to the Greeks of his day: 'For centuries you have been talking about the mind of God. *If you want to see what the mind of God is like, look at Jesus.*'

So then for me the supreme truth of Christianity is that in Jesus I see God. When I see Jesus feeding the hungry, comforting the sorrowing, befriending men and women with whom no one else would have had anything to do, I can say: 'This is God.'

It is not that Jesus *is* God. Time and time again the Fourth Gospel speaks of God sending Jesus into the world.

Time and time again we see Jesus praying to God. Time
and time again we see Jesus unhesitatingly and unquestion-
ingly and unconditionally accepting the will of God for
himself. Nowhere does the New Testament *identify* Jesus
and God. Jesus did not say: 'He who has seen me has seen
God.' He said: 'He who has seen me has seen *the Father.*'
There are attributes of God I do not see in Jesus. I do not
see God's omniscience in Jesus, for there are things which
Jesus did not know. I do not see God's omnipotence in Jesus
for there are things which Jesus could not do. I do not
see God's omnipresence in Jesus, for in his days on earth
Jesus could only be in one place at any given time. But in
Jesus I see perfectly and completely and finally, and once
and for all revealed and demonstrated, the attitude of God
to men, the attitude of God to me. In Jesus there is the full
revelation of the mind and the heart of God. And what a
difference it means to know that God is like that!

But why in the end had Jesus to die? Where does the
Cross come into this? All through his life Jesus was saying
to men, and through him God was saying to men: 'I love
you like that.' When he healed the sick, and touched the
untouchable, and loved the unlovely and the unlovable, he
is saying: 'I love you like that.' When he endured the
insults and the injuries and the treacheries and the dis-
loyalties of men, he is saying to them: 'Nothing you can do
to me will ever stop me loving you.' When Peter denies and
Judas betrays, he is saying to them: 'Nothing you can do to
me will ever stop me loving you.' When they flog him and
nail him to the Cross he prays: 'Father, forgive them, for
they don't know what they are doing', and in that prayer
he is saying: 'You can flog me, you can crucify me. Nothing
you can do to me will ever stop me loving you.' If Jesus had
stopped somewhere before death, if he had gone so far but
not the length of dying on the Cross, he would have been
saying: 'There are limits beyond which I am not prepared to

go. There is something at which I draw the line.' But because he went to death he was saying: 'There is nothing in
all the world that you can do to me that will stop me
loving you. I love you like that.' And what Jesus says,
God says. Jesus reveals to men the illimitable, the uncon-
querable, the literally infinite love of God. It the cost Cross
to tell men of the love of God. The pain and the agony of the
Cross was the price that Jesus had to pay, the sacrifice he
had to make to set before men the love of God.

I did not always think of the Cross and of the death of
Jesus like this. Like most people brought up in an evangelical home I did not at first know that there was any other
way of thinking of the Atonement except in terms of
substitution, in terms of God laying on Jesus the punishment that should have been laid on me. I knew Mrs Cousin's
hymn:

> Jehovah lifted up his rod;
>   O Christ, it fell on thee!
> Thou wast sore stricken of thy God;
>   There's not one stroke for me.
>   Thy tears, they blood
>   Beneath it flowed;
>   Thy bruising healeth me.
>
> Jehovah bade his sword awake;
>   O Christ, it woke 'gainst thee!
> Thy blood the flaming blade must slake,
>   Thy heart its sheath must be.
>   All for my sake,
>   My peace to make;
>   Now sleeps that sword for me.

Of course, I felt the fascination of this. Anyone must feel it.
But there were things about it that left me unhappy. It

seemed to oppose God and Jesus, and to present me with a God who was out to punish me and a Jesus who was out to save me. I could understand how the child felt when she said: 'I love Jesus, but I hate God.' The whole conception seemed to me to imply—Mrs Cousin's hymn does not imply it, it states it—that something Jesus did changed the attitude of God, pacified God, appeased God, persuaded him to withhold the hand raised to strike. It seemed to me that the whole conception starts from the wrath of God, while the New Testament starts from the love of God. It was because he so loved the world that God sent his Son into the world (John 3.16). It was his love that God showed to us in the death of Christ for us while we were still sinners (Rom. 5.8). Never in the New Testament, never once, is God said to be reconciled to man; it is always man who is reconciled to God. We plead with you, says Paul, on behalf of Christ, be reconciled to God (2 Cor. 5.20).

Slowly it began to dawn on me that apart from the love of God there would have been no Atonement at all. And then I began to see the tremendous thing, the fact that Jesus came, not to change God's attitude to men, but to demonstrate God's attitude to men, to show men at the cost of the Cross what God is like. And then still later, when I had to study the New Testament, I came to see that this is precisely what John is saying—and what a difference! The God of terror became the God of love. It became the most natural thing in the world to seek the presence of God instead of running away from God.

Let us see this difference in operation. I have written of this again and again because I do not think that it can be stated too often. First of all, let us see the thing in Judaism. The angel of the Lord came to Manoah and his wife to tell them that their son Samson was to be born, and when Manoah realised who their heavenly visitor had been he said in terror: 'We shall surely die, for we have seen God' (Judg. 13.22). In Judaism to see God was, so they believed, to die. Now let us turn to the New Testament. No one has seen God; it is the only Son who has revealed him (John 1.18). And revealed him as what? 'He who has seen me has seen the Father' (John 14.9). And in what sense? Jesus called God Abba (Mark 14.36). It is by that name that we too may call God, that we are invited to call him, says Paul (Rom. 8.15; Gal. 4.6). And what does this word Abba mean? Abba is the word—to this day—by which a little Jewish boy or girl addresses his father in the home circle, in the family. Through the house the child would shout 'Abba!'— Daddy.

As Jeremias has pointed out, no one in the long history of human thought had ever thought of God like that. It is a far cry from the God whom it is death to approach to the God whose relationship to us is the relationship of a loving father to a little child.

Second, let us take the early Greek conception of God. In the old Greek mythology Prometheus was the supreme benefactor of man; he instructed man in architecture, astronomy, mathematics, writing, rearing cattle, navigation, medicine, the art of prophecy, working in metal and in every other art. The myth said that Prometheus had made man of clay, and, to give his clay life, stole fire from heaven to put into it. The result was that Zeus chained him to a rock in the middle of the ocean and prepared a vulture to tear out his liver, which grew again each night to be torn out again each day. The gods grudged man everything, and any god who became a benefactor of men incurred the divine wrath in its most savage manifestation. What a difference between that and the God and Father of our Lord Jesus Christ!

Third, let us take the conception of the God of Greek philosophy contemporary with the New Testament. Both the great school of philosophy, the Stoics and the Epicureans, held that the supreme good in life is *ataraxia*, which means serenity If that is true for man, how much more must it be true of God? In order to provide God with this *ataraxia*, they held that God must have *apatheia*. *Apatheia* is not apathy in the sense of indifference; it is the complete inability to feel anything at all. The being who has *apatheia* cannot know love or hate, but remains for ever completely insulated against all feeling. If any one can cause us sorrow or joy, it means that for that moment that person is greater than we are, because that person can have some influence over us. So the way to complete serenity is insulation against all feeling. When the Countess of Lyttelton's husband died J. M. Barrie wrote to her: 'If you had cared for him less, if he had been less worth caring for, the road would be less heavy-going. Joy has to be paid for.' Sorrow is the price of love. If we never allowed ourselves to care for any one then there would be no such thing as sorrow. So the Greeks conceived of a God who essentially was unable to care. What a difference from the God who so loved the world, from the Jesus who could be moved with compassion, who wept! The difference between the apathetic Greek God and the Christian God of love is as wide as infinity.

I believe in Jesus, because it is only through Jesus that I know God as the Friend and Father, in whose presence I can be at home without fear, as a child with his father.

I believe in life after death. I never begin to write or speak about this without my thoughts going back to an extra-mural class I had many years ago, before the war. We were discussing one evening the subject of the life to come, and a lady in the class not young, cultured, experienced, well-to-do, began the discussion by saying that the last thing she wanted was a life to come. She was tired, weary of life and living, and all she wanted was to cease to be. The famous Colonel T. E. Lawrence felt the same way.

'O Lord,' he said. 'I am so tired. I want to lie down to sleep, to die. To die is better because there is no reveillé.' It is as Swinburne wrote with his own haunting magic of words:

> From too much love of living,
>   From hope and fear set free,
> We thank with brief thanksgiving
>   Whatever gods may be
> That no man lives forever,
> That dead men rise up never,
> That even the weariest river
>   Winds somewhere safe to sea.

But in spite of that I think that most people want life. Achilles would have had this life go on. He would, he said, rather be a hired labourer on earth, working for a man of no substance, than king of all the dead. Plutarch says that the one thing the Greek could not bear to contemplate was annihilation; he would rather be tormented in hell than annihilated. Let us look at the arguments for life after death. We have done it often before—but it never does any harm to give faith some encouragement. Do you remember Thomas Hardy's poem, *The Oxen*? The country folk have a thought that on Christmas Eve at twelve o'clock the animals kneel in their stalls, in memory of the wondrous birth in a stable so many years ago. The poem ends with Hardy saying that, if some one told him that in the lonely farm that very night the animals were kneeling in the straw, and asked him to come to see the sight,

> I should go with him in the gloom,
>   Hoping it might be so.

I think that in regard to the life to come, even for the best of us, sometimes it is gazing through the gloom, and hoping it might be so. That is why—for my own sake—I stop to look at the old arguments again.

All arguments for a life to come must begin from the
nature of God. It is only because we believe in the God who
is the God and Father of our Lord Jesus Christ that we
believe in a life to come. Thomas Hardy spoke of 'the dream-
ing, dark, dumb thing that turns the handle of the idle
show'. In the unforgettable phrase he wrote the famous
epitaph: 'The President of the Immortals (in Aeschylean
phrase) had ended his sport with Tess.' No one would
easily believe in a life to come believing in a God like that.
Bertrand Russell imagines how God, weary of the angels,
made men. He surrounded men with tears and troubles and
man reacted gallantly, and God watched with a certain
amusement. Then God grew tired of watching. 'A good
play!' he said. 'Some day I must do it again! Meanwhile—
enough! The jest is ended!' And with a sweep of his hand
he annihilated man. As Shakespeare had it in *King Lear*:

> As flies to wanton boys, are we to the gods;
> They kill us for their sport.

Again, no one could easily believe in a life to come, believing in a God like that. But in the God whom Jesus came to
reveal there are two qualities which make a life to come a
necessity in the divine scheme of things. There is *the
justice of God*. No one can say that in this world virtue
gains its reward and wickedness its punishment. If there is
to be any justice in life, a new world must be called in to
redress the balance of the old. There is *the love of God*. In
this world young lives are cut off too soon, and often in a
way that just does not make sense. If there is no place in
which these lives receive their chance to flourish, to blossom
in their beauty, to realise their potential, to be what this
life never allowed them to be, then it is not love which is at
the centre of this world.

The second argument is from the nature of man. I
told you that from the point of view of philosophy I am

simple-minded. I am still impressed by Kant's teleological argument, from the assumption that man has a *telos*, an end, which he is created, designed to reach. The highest good is absolute obedience to the moral law. Such obedience is virtue. This is a truth which is laid down by reason. Further, reason lays it down that the completest good is when virtue and happiness are united. But, if virtue is perfect obedience to the moral law, it is unobtainable; it cannot be obtained in any finite period, because of the opposition of man's animal and passional nature to the moral imperative. The complete good, the union of virtue and happiness, is not realisable in this life. Therefore, a life to come is a necessity, if man is ever to be what reason says he ought to be, if he is to complete his *telos*, the end for which he was created and designed. To complete that *telos* this life is not enough. Therefore there must be another life still to come, when the *telos* will be reached. Man never realises himself, or God's design for him, unless there is a life to come.

The third argument is from the nature of life. Here is the famous argument which Plato worked out in the *Phaedo*. Plato used three main arguments. First, everything is generated from its opposite. You can't have hot unless you have cold; you can't have strong unless you have weak. So you cannot have life unless you have death. But if the movement was all in one direction, in the direction of life to death, then there would be no life left. So the process must work in the other direction also; life must generate death, and death must generate life; and so the process of life and death goes on. Second, Plato made much of the doctrine of reminiscence. That is to say, he believed that we do not discover things: we remember them. For instance in one of his dialogues he shows Socrates extracting from a totally uneducated slave boy the proof of the twenty-ninth theorem of Euclid, the theorem of Pythagoras, that the square on the hypotenuse of a right-angled triangle equals the sum of the squares on the other two sides, simply by question and answer. The boy had never learned it; he must have remembered it. When we say that two pieces of wood are *equal*, where do we get the idea of equal? We don't learn it—we must remember it. So Plato argues that if knowledge is really reminiscence, then the soul must be pre-existent and will go on existing. Third, Plato argues from the exclusion of opposites. A thing cannot be hot and cold at the same time, neither can it have the characteristics of cold—for example, snow—when it is hot. The characteristic of the soul is life. Therefore, death is excluded. Such are the Platonic arguments. I do not think that they would beget faith, but they may well support a faith that is already there.

So then I believe in the life to come, not because of the proofs of the philosophers, but because the whole teaching of the New Testament is based on the assumption that there is life after death.

But in one thing I would go beyond strict orthodoxy—I am a convinced universalist. I believe that in the end all men will be gathered into the love of God. In the early days Origen was the great name connected with universalism. I would believe with Origen that universalism is no easy thing. Origen believed that after death there were many who would need prolonged instruction, the sternest discipline, even the severest punishment before they were fit for the presence of God. Origen did not eliminate hell; he believed that some people would have to go to heaven via hell. He believed that even at the end of the day there would be some on whom the scars remained. He did not believe in eternal *punishment*, but he did see the possibility of eternal *penalty*. And so the choice is whether we accept God's offer and invitation willingly, or take the long and terrible way round through ages of purification.

Gregory of Nyssa offered three reasons why he believed in universalism. First, he believed in it because of *the character of God*. 'Being good, God entertains pity for fallen man; being wise, he is not ignorant of the means for his recovery.' Second, he believed in it because of *the nature of evil*. Evil must in the end be moved out of existence, 'so that the absolutely non-existent should cease to be at all'. Evil is essentially negative and doomed to non-existence. Third, he believed in it because of *the purpose of punishment*. The purpose of punishment is always remedial. Its aim is 'to get the good separated from the evil and to attract it into the communion of blessedness'. Punishment will hurt, but it is like the fire which separates the alloy from the gold; it is like the surgery which removes the diseased thing; it is like the cautery which burns out that which cannot be removed any other way.

But I want to set down not the arguments of others but the thoughts which have persuaded me personally of universal salvation.

First, there is the fact that there are things in the New Testament which more than justify this belief. Jesus said: 'I, when I am lifted up from the earth, will draw *all* men to myself' (John 12.32). Paul writes to the Romans: 'God has consigned *all* men to disobedience that he may have mercy on *all*' (Rom. 11.32). He writes to the Corinthians: 'As in Adam *all* die, so also in Christ shall *all* be made alive' (1 Cor. 15.22); and he looks to the final total triumph when God will be everything to everyone (1 Cor. 15.28). In the First Letter to Timothy we read of God 'who desires *all* men to be saved and to come to the knowledge of the truth', and of Christ Jesus 'who gave himself as a ransom for *all*' (1 Tim. 2.4-6). The New Testament itself is not in the least afraid of the word *all*.

Second, one of the key passages is Matthew 25.46 where it is said that the rejected go away to *eternal punishment*, and the righteous to eternal life. The Greek word for punishment is *kolasis*, which was not originally an ethical word at all. It originally meant the pruning of trees to make them grow better. I think it is true to say that in all Greek secular literature *kolasis* is never used of anything but remedial punishment. The word for eternal is *aiōnios*. It means more than everlasting, for Plato—who may have invented the word—plainly says that a thing may be everlasting and still not be *aiōnios*. The simplest way to put it is that *aiōnios* cannot be used properly of anyone but God; it is the word uniquely, as Plato saw it, of God. Eternal punishment is then literally that kind of remedial punishment which it befits God to give and which only God can give.

Third, I believe that it is impossible to set limits to the grace of God. I believe that not only in this world, but in any other world there may be, the grace of God is still effective, still operative, still at work. I do not believe that the operation of the grace of God is limited to this world. I believe that the grace of God is as wide as the universe.

Fourth, I believe implicitly in the ultimate and complete triumph of God, the time when all things will be subject to him, and when God will be everything to everyone (1 Cor. 15.24–28). For me this has certain consequences. If one man remains outside the love of God at the end of time, it means that that one man has defeated the love of God—and that is impossible. Further, there is only one way in which we can think of the triumph of God. If God was no more than a King or Judge, then it would be possible to speak of his triumph, if his enemies were agonising in hell or were totally and completely obliterated and wiped out. But God is not only King and Judge, God is *Father*—he is indeed Father more than anything else. No father could be happy while there were members of his family for ever in agony. No father would count it a triumph to obliterate the

disobedient members of his family. The only triumph a
father can know is to have all his family back home. The
only victory love can enjoy is the day when its offer of love
is answered by the return of love. The only possible final
triumph is a universe loved by and in love with God.

Two objections are commonly levelled against universalism. It is claimed that it takes the iron out of Christianity
because it removes the threat. No longer can the sinner be
dangled over the pit of hell. No longer can what Burns
called 'the hangman's whip' of the fear of hell be threaten-
ingly cracked over the sinner. But the kind of universalism
in which I believe has not simply obliterated hell and said
that everything will be all right for everyone; it has stated
grimly that, if you will have it so, you can go to heaven via
hell. The threat is still there. Further, it is claimed that
universalism does away with free-will. Early on in his
thought Origen has the astonishing picture of a universe in
which the free-will always obtains and in which to the end
of time a man can fall from heaven and rise from hell;
but in the end he came to think in terms of a final decision.
What is forgotten is that God has eternity to work in. It
is not a question of God, as it were, rushing a man into
heaven. It is a question of God using an eternity of per-
suasion and appeal until the hardest heart breaks down and
the most stubborn sinner repents.

As I see it, nothing less than a world is enough for the
love of God.

When you think about death, there are certain things
which insist on coming into the mind. There is the fear of
death. The writer to the Hebrews spoke of those 'who
through fear of death were subject to lifelong bondage'
(Heb. 2.15). I often feel that Julius and Augustus Hare had
something when they said: 'The ancients dreaded death;
the Christian can only fear dying.' What so many fear is not
death, it is the process of dying, the pain, the humiliation,

the general messiness, which attend life when this body has a slow progress to decay. H. G. Wells has a passage in his Autobiography. His father, grandfather, elder brother all dropped dead in the middle of a sentence. Wells goes on to say:

> There is an irregularity in our family pulse: it misses a beat ever and again, and sooner or later it misses more than one beat and that is the end of us . . . I shall hate to leave the spectacle of life, but go I must at last, and I hope when my time is fulfilled that I too may depart in this apparently hereditary manner. It seems to me that, whatever other defects we have, we have an admirable way of dying.

It is told that, when he was asked what kind of death he would desire, Julius Caesar answered: 'A sudden one.' I think that it may well be that we are less afraid of death than we are afraid of the discomfort of dying.

There is the constantly recurring question whether we shall know and meet and recognize each other again on the other side of death. One thing is quite certain—Christian orthodoxy does not teach the immortality of the soul; it teaches the resurrection of the body. We do not mean by that the resurrection of this body as it is. For many of us the last thing in the world that we would want is the resurrection of the burden and the weariness of this mortal body. We would never wish for the resurrection of the actual body with which a man was smashed up in an accident or died with an incurable disease. It so happens that Greek has no no word for personality, and the resurrection of the body means the survival of the personality; it means that in the life beyond, you will still be you, and I will still be I. This is in opposition, for instance, to the beliefs of Stoicism. The Stoics believed that God is a fire, more pure than any earthly fire; and what gives man life is that a spark, a *scintilla*, of the divine fire comes and lives in his body. When he dies, the spark of divine fire, goes back to its source and is reabsorbed in the life of all things, in the being of God. That is the immortality of the soul, but it is not the survival of personality.

In 1928 the *Daily News* had a series of articles on 'Where are the Dead?' to which George Bernard Shaw was asked to contribute. Shaw complained that the contributors had treated the whole matter as if it was a philosophic abstraction. And that way of treating it 'takes our feet off the earth so completely as to enable the controversialists to prove that there may be such a thing as immortality without producing the faintest conviction that any particular Tom, Dick or Harry, Susan, Sophronia or Jane ever was or will be immortal'. He goes on:

> What I propose is that your next few contributors shall discuss, not whether 'we' are immortal, or whether the soul is immortal, or whether the dead are still seeking lodgings in infinite space, but whether I, Bernard Shaw, am going to persist to all eternity in a universe utterly unable to get rid of me, no matter how desperately tired it may become of the Shavianismus, or how intolerably bored I may be by myself.

He concludes:

> When I use the word 'I' (as I frequently do), I mean myself, with all my imperfections (if any) on my head, and my eyebrows turning up, and not down like those of my friend Mr George Robey. I mean the celebrated G.B.S., almost unbearably individualised, with his consciousness and his memories, his tricks and his manners, complete and exact in his G.B. Essence. Otherwise the controversy is about nothing.

Of course, Shaw was right. It is not about the abstraction

of the immortality of the soul that we are talking; it is
about the resurrection of the body, the survival of personality, the continued existence of you and me.

This means that in the beyond we will meet each other
again. But I have never been able to see in this only the
joy of meeting again those whom we have loved and lost
awhile. We shall have to meet again those whom we have
wronged; those to whom we have been disloyal; those
whom we have hurt; those whom we have deceived. There
will be no doubt the reuniting of love, but there will also be
confrontation with truth. The one thing that haunted Paul
long after he had become an apostle was that he had been a
persecutor (Gal. 1.13; 1 Cor. 15.9; Phil. 3.6; 1 Tim. 1.13).
'When they were put to death,' he said of the Christians,
'I cast my vote against them' (Acts 26.10). He was a
participant in the lynching of Stephen (Acts 7.58; 8.1).
F. W. H. Myers makes Paul think of this in his poem
'Saint Paul', as he remembers the deaths of the saints for
which he was responsible:

> Saint, did I say? With your remembered faces,
>> Dear men and women whom I sought and slew!
> Ah when we mingle in the heavenly places
>> How will I weep to Stephen and to you!

The meetings again will have their joy, but they will also
have their shame, but we can hope and believe that in the
heavenly places those who have been forgiven will also
learn to forgive.

One last thing comes to mind, when we think of life and
of its ending—and that is the funeral which will write finis
to the last chapter. I have always wished that when my
time comes there should be no funeral service whatsoever.
I should like my dead body to be cremated with no service
at all; I should like my ashes to be scattered in one of the
places that I loved by the moors and the sea, again with no

service and no ceremony. I shall be gladly done with my body—and I do not care what they do with it. I would have my loved ones spared the public ordeal which a funeral service must be. I have always felt that at our funeral services there is something very like the worship of death, whereas if we were logical it would be a time of rejoicing that our loved one had passed from death to life. In Thomas Hardy's book *The Mayor of Casterbridge* Michael Henchard's will is set out:

> That Elizabeth-Jane Farfrae be not told of my death, or made to grieve on account of me,
> & that I be not buried in consecrated ground,
> & that no sexton be asked to toll the bell,
> & that nobody is wished to see the dead body,
> & that no mourners walk behind me at my funeral,
> & that no flowers be planted on my grave,
> & that no man remember me.
> To this I put my name.

I too would put my name to that. When I die, I should like to slip out of the room without fuss—for what matters is not what I am leaving, but where I am going.

And last, among all the religious and theological 'believes' I want to set at the end what is for me the biggest 'believe' of all: I believe in the home; I believe in marriage; I believe in the family.

There always has been a line of thought which held that for the man who wants to be a real thinker, a real philosopher, a real scholar, marriage is fatal. When Epictetus is describing the perfect Cynic, the perfect philosopher, he says that it is a question

> if the Cynic ought not to be free from distraction, wholly devoted to the service of God, free to go about among men, not tied down by the private duties of men, nor involved in relationships which he cannot violate and

still maintain his role as a good and excellent man, whereas, on the other hand, if he observes them, he will destroy the messenger, the scout, the herald of the gods that he is. For see, he must show certain services to his father-in-law, to the rest of his wife's relatives, to his wife herself; finally, he is driven from his profession, to act as a nurse to his own family and to provide for them. To make a long story short, he must get a kettle to heat water for the baby, for washing it in a bathtub; wool for his wife when she has had a child, a cot, a cup (the vessels get more and more numerous); not to speak of the rest of his business and his distraction.

Where is the man who is tied down to the duties of everyday life to find leisure for such matters (philosophy)? Come, doesn't he have to get little cloaks for the children? Doesn't he have to send them off to a schoolteacher with their little tablets and writing implements, and little note-books; and besides get the little cot ready for them?

If the philosopher is charged with failing in his duty to posterity, his answer is that by devoting himself to philosophy he is doing far more than he would have done, if he had brought 'two or three dirty-nosed children' into the world. For Epictetus marriage and a family were the destruction of a philosopher.

The story of Heloise and Abelard is more than eight hundred years old, but to this day it is one of the supreme love-stories of the world. Heloise was only seventeen years old, a rarity for these days, a beautiful girl who was also a scholar. Abelard, the brilliant scholar and teacher, succeeded in becoming her tutor. He seduced her. She was with child. He would have married her—in the end he did, only for her to go straight into a convent. But the last thing she wanted was marriage. For herself, she desired to be bound to Abelard by the bond of love and love alone. 'The term "wife" may seem to you holier and more substantial, but another was always dearer to my heart, that of your mistress, or even—allow me to say it—of your concubine, your whore.' 'As God is my witness, had Augustus. the master of the world, adjuged me worthy of marriage, and had his sovereignty of the universe been assured for ever, being known as your courtesan would have seemed sweeter and nobler to me than being known as his empress.' She felt that any other obligation than love alone would ruin everything. For Abelard, she could not bear to think of marriage. 'Think of the situation wedlock would inflict upon you. What connection can there be between scholarship and running a house, between a desk and a cradle, a book or tablet and a distaff, a pen or stylus and a spindle? Is there anywhere a man who, with his mind on Scripture or philosophy, can endure the wailings of a new-born child, the songs of the nurse lulling it to sleep, the comings and goings of the household staff, the dirtiness of early infancy?' As Régine Pernoud says: 'She could not bear to think of this exceptional man reduced to the level of a domesticated husband and father.' To Heloise it was impossible that Abelard should continue to be Abelard and undertake the duties of a home.

In modern times Cyril Conolly passed the remark: 'There is no more sombre enemy of good art than the pram in the hall.'

I feel exactly the opposite of all this. If I have done anything in the world, every single item of it is due to my home. Home is the only place in the world where it is possible to relax. In Robert Frost's *The Death of the Hired Man* there is a conversation:

> 'Home is the place where, when you have to go there,
> They take you in.'

'I should have called it
Something you somehow don't have to deserve.'

What you've done or what you haven't done, the labels, the
honours, the degrees—they have nothing to do with home.
It is where you can come just because you are you. J. M.
Barrie wrote a letter to Lady Cynthia Asquith who was for
so long his secretary: 'I think that to be brave all the time
is more than should be demanded of you, however gallantly
you stand up to it, and you are indeed a marvel at it.'
Home is the place where you don't need to be brave. Home
is the place where they know us at our worst and still love
us. I believe in home—I believe in marriage—I believe in
the family, for I could not have lived without them.

4

THE DAY'S WORK

Hugh Martin in his book *The Parables of the Gospels* tells us that his old teacher Sir Henry Jones used to say that the most pathetic line in all Shakespeare was this: 'Othello's occupation's gone.' Five months from now my occupation will be gone, and, since the long vacation forms a large part of these months, I have only five weeks of teaching left to do. So it is a good time to stand and look back on the day's work over these more than forty years. My work has lain in three spheres.

I began by being the pastor of a congregation. I can honestly say that that part of my work was the most difficult and exhausting that I ever had to do, and at the same time the most satisfying, even if it was also the most humiliating in that it could have been done so very much better. The ministry involves two main activities.

It involves the pastoral care of the congregation. Early on in my ministry, and in some ways even to the end of it, I dreaded pastoral visitation. In *Courage to Change* June Bingham wrote the biography of Reinhold Niebuhr. In it she quotes a letter from Niebuhr to his mother in the very early days of his ministry:

I am glad there are only 18 families in this church. I have been visiting the members for six weeks and haven't seen all of them yet. Usually I walk past a house two or three times before I summon the courage to go in. I am always very courteously received, so I don't know exactly why I should not be able to overcome this curious timidity.

I used to feel much the same. It was not that I do not like people; I do. It was the feeling of responsibility. The trouble is that the pastor's visit should be more than a social call, but at the same time it should not be a kind of ordeal for the household. Fortunately it is somehow true that in an amazingly short time the man becomes the minister. Even when a man is no more than twenty-three or twenty-four, just because he is the minister, people will open their minds and hearts to him, and tell him of their most intimate spiritual and even physical troubles. The minister, even when he is little more than a boy, acquires a status which is not his own.

But this is just the problem. I believe that before a man can talk to another person about the deep things of life, he must establish a certain human relationship with that person. I do not think that a man has the right to go up to a total stranger and demand: 'Are you saved?' any more than he has the right to go up and ask him about the state of his bank account. A relationship has to be arrived at in which it is possible to talk of these things. But the great and grave danger is to lose the chance of taking about them at all.

I once heard one of the greatest chaplains the British Army ever had tell a story about that great soldier Field Marshal Slim. The thing happened in the Burma campaign. Slim asked the senior chaplain to arrange for a visit to one of his soldiers who was going through a bad time. News had come to Burma that his wife was behaving, to say the least of it, indiscreetly at home. The chaplain was duly sent to see the man. After the visit Slim sent for the senior chaplain. 'Padre,' he said, 'about that visit I asked you to get one of your chaplains to pay.' 'Well, sir,' said the senior chaplain, 'what about it?' 'Well, padre,' said Slim, 'your chaplain went to see the man. He was very nice to him. He smoked a cigarette with him, and drank a cup of tea with him. But he never showed that soldier the one thing he wanted to see.' 'What was that?' said the senior chaplain. And Slim answered: 'The man on the Cross.' 'Padre,' said Slim, 'when are you going to show us the one thing we want to see—the man on the Cross?' Don't mistake me. I'm not saying that at every visit the minister must talk religion; I'm not saying that at every visit he must say a prayer. But I am saying that somehow or other he must acquire the spiritual awareness which will enable him to see when these things have to be spoken about, And there lies the problem—and the problem is the terrible possibility of failing your people just when they need you most, and of paying a social visit, when they want the man on the Cross.

As I have already said, I had a long ministry in the one place, and over the years a pastor is bound to grow close to his people. And just sometimes something happens which shows that in the ministry you never know what you are doing. I still have a letter dated 2 March 1945. It is from a boy who was called up to be a soldier. He wrote to me like this:

During the last few weeks I have thought much. God and Christ I have sincerely believed in, but the Church has always stumped me. I looked for faults and saw only faults. Now I can honestly say I look on the Church in a different light . . . I must admit there are still many points I can't see eye to eye with, but they are of little importance. Next Sunday I shall take the oath, stating that I believe in God and in Christ, and that I shall strive to uphold his Church with all my power. I pray to God that I shan't fail.

It is something to get a letter like that from a boy whose daily business was to face death, and to know that the Sunday School and the Bible Class did not go for nothing. It is something to get letters from the other side of the world from men and women who were boys and girls in Renfrew thirty or forty years ago, and who have still not forgotten.

I said that the pastoral side of the ministry was often a terror and an agony, but when I left the parish ministry and went to teach in a university one of the things that I missed most of all and still miss is the circle of nearly a thousand homes into the fellowship of which the pastor was always welcome.

The second thing that the ministry involves is preaching, and all my life I have regarded preaching with dread. Howard Williams, the minister of Bloomsbury Baptist Church, himself a notable preacher, says in his book on preaching, *My Word*: 'No man in his senses would choose to be a preacher.' Dr Williams tells us that it was Paul Tillich's habit 'to approach a pulpit with fear and trembling'. This I can well understand. Some preachers insist on being left alone before a service: I was always the opposite. I needed someone to be with me in those minutes before the service began.

For me to enter a pulpit has always been a literally terrifying experience. It is a comfort to find that other people in similar circumstances have felt the same way. It is, I think, in fact true, that, if a man can enter a pulpit without turning a hair, then it is time that he stopped entering it. In his Warrack lectures on preaching, *In Christ's Stead*, A. J. Gossip, that prince of preachers, my old teacher, writes:

When I was still at New College, Whyte asked me to preach in St George's; and the time being far ahead, and being flattered, I consented, although when the thing drew near I struggled desperately to escape, in vain. It was a very wretched youth that crept into the pulpit, and his discomfiture was made complete by seeing Rainy in the congregation. That great soul walked home part of the way with me and, among other things, said this: 'You chose a great subject. That was right. You cannot always do it. But do it as often as you can.' That, I believe, was very sound advice, though it is not the easy path. So long as we are pirouetting with some pretty bit of a text on the outskirts of things, we feel fairly easy in our minds. But it is a very humbled creature who stands up to preach on some tremendous central passage such as 'God so loved the world'. Well, to begin with, we are likelier, I take it, to be used in that mood than when we are feeling fairly cocksure.

He is a strangely insensitive creature who can stand without awe in the presence of God and bearing his people on his heart.

The great 'performers'—if you will forgive the word—have been the terrified performers. W. H. Elliott, once famous as one of radio's greatest preachers, tells in his book, *Undiscovered Ends*, how he was in the company of Forbes Robertson the great actor just before Robertson was about to give a recital at Folkstone Literary Society. The great actor was in a state bordering on collapse. 'Don't worry,' he said to Elliott, 'I am always like this before I go on. I always feel "green".' Robert Dougal, the famous broadcaster, tells in his autobiography, *In and Out of the Box*, how he felt the day he began the Empire broadcast transmission:

Then the morning came when I was on my own, alone with the Empire in Studio 7A. Sitting in that tiny studio where I was to spend so many hours round the clock in

the next few years, I was sweating with fear . . . The
current pop tune was Jerome Kern's 'Smoke gets in your
eyes', and a very good one too, but as far as I was con-
cerned the trouble was sweat running down my arm-pits.
Not from heat, but sheer terror.

Later in the television days of his career Robert Dougall
says;

The television news editor of these days, S. W. 'Pat'
Smithers, described my early performances like this:
'The top half of you on the screen looks all right, Bob,
but I keep wondering what's happening to your legs
under the table.' I knew just what he meant. In fact my
legs were tying themselves in knots.

Richard Baker, an equally famous broadcaster, tells us:
'Occasionally, just before the news, I think to myself:
"Oh God, I can't do it again." I have to control the panic
and stop myself breaking into a cold sweat.' After Ian
Ramsey had left his Oxford chair to become Bishop of
Durham, he used to say, as David L. Edwards tells us in
Ian Ramsey, Bishop of Durham, A Memoir, that it was
more difficult to prepare a parochial sermon than a university lecture. I have always been haunted by the sheer dread
of preaching, and yet I would not have it otherwise. When
to preach becomes a commonplace, then it is time to stop
preaching.

If you count the years when I began to preach as a student,
I have been preaching for something like forty-five years;
and in these years I have come to certain conclusions about
preaching.

(i) I want to begin at what some people will regard as a
very low level. A great deal of the effect of preaching
depends on technique. Technique is not a popular word
with so-called spiritually-minded people. But the art of
cooking bears a very close analogy to the art of preaching.

All cooks use exactly the same ingredients, but out of these ingredients one will produce a most appetising and attractive meal, and another will produce a revolting and uneatable mess; the difference is in the technique. All preachers use the same material, the Bible and the doctrines of the Christian faith; and yet one will rivet the attention and another will produce sleep. The difference will often lie in the technique. Let no budding preacher ever despise teaching on how to preach. There was a time when universities appointed their professors and lecturers on the strength of their academic qualifications and the excellence of their published work. They seldom made any enquiry as to whether the man was able to communicate his own knowledge to the students he had to teach. It is very significant that universities are now laying on courses on how to teach for new members of their staffs and are insisting that these courses be taken. If a man wishes to be a preacher or a teacher, it will profit him and his hearers nothing, if he has all the knowledge in the world, but is quite unable to transmit it.

Marcus Dods, the famous Scottish teacher and preacher, used to insist that on many occasions when people said that a sermon was a good sermon, it meant no more than they had been able to *hear* it. There are few of us who do not have speaking habits of one kind or another, and sometimes these habits are such that they detract from the effectiveness of our preaching or our teaching. Happy is the man who has a loving wife or a wise friend who will tell him if it is so with him.

In New Testament times the Jewish synagogue service ended with the Aaronic blessing: 'The Lord bless you and keep you; the Lord make his face to shine upon you, and be gracious to you; the Lord lift up his countenance upon you, and give you peace' (Num. 6.24–26). That blessing was to be pronounced by a priest, if a priest was present. But there was a regulation that it must not be pronounced by a Galilean or by a person whose fingers were stained, and on whose hand the stain could be seen when he raised it in the act of blessing. The Galileans spoke with a characteristic burr. At the trial of Jesus, Peter in the courtyard of the high priest's house was recognized as a Galilean, because his accent gave him away (Matt. 26.73). The point of the Jewish regulation was that nothing must distract the attention of the worshipper from the blessing, and if there was anything about the person pronouncing it calculated so to distract, then he was debarred from doing so. We begin with the simple fact that, if a man has a message to give, it will be essential for him to learn the best way of presenting that message, and to see to it that there is nothing in him which will act as a barrier to the message. In other words, if he despises technique, he will be a very foolish man.

(ii) To turn now to things which are at a deeper level, preaching must be by compulsion. I have already quoted Howard Williams' saying that no man in his senses would choose to be a preacher, but he goes straight on to say:

> Let preaching become a work to be avoided except by those who believe they must do it. Constraint has been a mark of preaching since Moses became aware of his stammering tongue and Jeremiah felt the fire in his bones.

As Paul said long ago: 'Necessity is laid upon me. Woe to me if I do not preach the gospel!' (I Cor. 9.16). Preaching cannot be a spare-time hobby, or a pleasant side-line. The preacher is the man who speaks because he cannot keep silent.

(iii) This is another way of saying that preaching must be by conviction. The listener will always know when a man believes intensely in what he says, and even if the listener does not agree, even if he thinks the speaker is misguided, he respects the accent of conviction. Howard Williams quotes the words of a famous Welshman called Thomas Jones. Thomas Jones had left Wales when he was a very young man. He had been connected closely with the great events in the history of the nation. Then late in life he returned to Wales, and in a lecture given in 1942 he said:

I have usually heard a sermon every Sunday since my return to Wales. Of the scores of sermons I have listened to I should say not half a dozen have given me any sense of an urgent message for the congregation; that it mattered profoundly whether the preacher delivered it or not; that there was anything more than that it was to be deplored that the nations were at war and that it was hoped that God would bring peace soon to a stricken world. Most of the sermons are essays, lectures, talks, sometimes with a pleasant literary flavour.

There is a strange saying of Jesus in the Gospels: 'The good news of the kingdom of God is preached, and everyone enters it violently' (Luke 16.16; cp. Matt. 11.12). I think that it was James Denney who commented on that saying: 'The kingdom of God is not for the well-meaning, but for the desperate.' Very often what is left after a sermon will not be something hard and definite; it will be an impression. Gossip in *In Christ's Stead* writes:

My father used to tell of an excited man, standing beside him in the Waverley Market, when Gladstone was speaking, to whom even that wonderful voice failed to penetrate, yet he kept crying in a kind of ecstasy: 'It's grand, grand, though I canna hear one word of it.'

It is perfectly intelligible that a man not hearing, or not understanding should still have the impression, the feeling, that something tremendous is at stake. The plain fact is that unless the preacher or teacher can give the impression

77

that what he is talking about matters to himself, he will certainly not make it matter to anyone else.

(iv) Preaching must be derived from experience. This is the other side of the necessity of technique. W. H. Elliott in *Undiscovered Ends* tells how he once heard the famous pianist Cortot play Chopin's B Minor Sonata in which there is the famous Funeral March. After the performance Elliott said to Cortot: 'How superb! I never heard anything like it!' And Cortot replied: 'You see I felt it so much. This week I lost a very dear friend!' The perfect performance comes when the deep experience meets the perfect technique.

There is an obvious problem here. Experience is not something which can be commanded. The flow of experience cannot be turned on and off like a tap. The hot-blooded man will have experiences which the man with a cool, calm, passionless temperament cannot share. Youth will not have the same experience as age. It is, for instance, difficult, perhaps impossible, to feel the real impact of the belief in life after death, until some one we love has died. Theology is not simply a thing of thought; we learn as much theology as life teaches us. On the other hand no man has any right to preach as if his own experience is the norm for all experience and the only experience there is. Nevertheless, any preacher ought to aim to bring to his people the full orb of Christian truth. That is to say, and to this we will soon return, he should preach his way through the whole creed and through the whole body of Christian doctrine. If he does that two things at least will happen. First, he himself will know, and his people will know, what the Church does believe, and second, it happens to be a fact that the very study of some doctrine, the very effort to understand it, always leads some way along the path to experiencing it. If a man feels that there is some doctrine which means very little to him, and which is outside his experience, it is that very doctrine he should study and seek to expound, and out of the study will come experience, and in explaining it to others he will grasp it himself.

(v) Preaching ought to be biblically and credally centred This is far from saying that preaching should never deal with the social, political and economic situation, but it is to say that it should start from the Christian book and the Christian belief. Gossip, in *In Christ's Stead*, quotes an outburst of that famous preacher Robertson of Brighton:

> I wish I did not hate preaching so much, but the degradation of being a Brighton preacher is almost intolerable. I do not depreciate spiritual work; I hold it higher than secular; all I say and feel is that by the change of times the pulpit has lost its place. It does only part of that whole that used to be done by it alone. Once it was newspaper, schoolmaster, theological treatise, a stimulant to good work, historical lecture, metaphysics, etc., all in one. Now these are partitioned out to different officers, and the pulpit is no more the pulpit of three centuries ago than the authority of the master of a household is that of Abraham who was soldier, butcher, sacrificer, shepherd and emir in one person.

There is a good deal of truth in that. The basic truth is that there was a time when the parson was the only educated man in the parish, a time before compulsory education, before higher education was opened to all, before cheap, mass produced books, before newspapers which do far more than merely record news, before wireless and television. The general public are now much more widely informed than they used to be; the Church no longer has a monopoly of education. For the parson this means that people are no longer very interested in his opinions about politics, or economics, or science. The only special expertise that he possesses is that he is skilled in the interpretation

of the Bible and of the Christian faith. It is to expound
the Bible and explain and commend the faith that he is
trained. This is the special and particular skill which
distinguishes him from other men. This is the one sphere in
which he can speak with authority. His duty is therefore
in the first place to expound the Bible and the Christian
faith, and then, and only then, to apply the principles thus
extracted to the individuals to whom he is preaching, to the
community in which they are resident, to the country of
which they are citizens, to the world situation at large. In
other words, to put it in summary but technical language,
there has been far too much topical preachng and far too
little expository preaching. The preacher should at least
begin by doing the one thing that he is qualified to do.

(iv) To return now to a point which we have already made
in prinicple—preaching ought to be systematic. A look at
any pulpit Bible will show how comparatively small an
amount of the Bible we actually read. There are pages
which are worn and brown with continual use—Psalms
23, 46, 102, 145, Isaiah 35 and 53, most of the Gospels,
Romans 8, 1 Corinthians 13—while there are great tracts
of the Bible where the pages still have their virgin whitencss
and which are obviously unused. In New Testament times
in the synagogue the Old Testament was read according to
a lectionary, which took the congregation right through
it once either in one year or in three years. There is
everything to be said for that. One of the most dangerous
things a preacher can do is to make his own preferences
the decisive factor in what he preaches. Again and again
it has been my own experience that I thought that some
New Testament book had no special interest for me, and
for years I neglected it. Then for some reason or other I
had to make a study of it, and the more I studied it the
more interesting it became, so that often books which I
had once neglected became favourite books. Systematic

preaching will bring the congregation face to face with the whole of Scripture, and it will also have the not unimportant advantage that the preacher will have his subject prescribed for him in advance, and there will be no last minute search for something to preach about.

(vii) There would be another way to put this as a general principle—preaching should be to a very large extent teaching. There are four Greek words for four different kinds of preaching. There is *kērugma*. *Kērugma* means a herald's proclamation, and it is the announcement without argument of that which is most surely believed. It is the plain, uncompromising statement of Christian belief. There is *didachē*. *Didachē* means teaching. Suppose some one says: 'So what?' If we can tell them the 'so what', the meaning and the relevance of what *kērugma* has stated, that is teaching. There is *paraklēsis*. *Paraklēsis* means exhortation, and it is the appeal to the hearer to accept and to act upon what the teaching has laid down. There is *homilia*. *Homilia* is the treatment of any subject in the light of the Christian message. It may be not entirely untrue to say that a very great deal of modern preaching is *paraklēsis*, exhortation; but it is entirely obvious that there is no point in exhorting people to be Christians until they know what being Christian means. And this is to say that there is an urgent need for a return to a teaching ministry.

(viii) A teaching ministry must of necessity be a learning ministry. No man can continue to give out, unless he also takes in. It is to be noted that I did not use the phrase an educated ministry, or an informed ministry; I used the phrase a *learning* ministry, and I used the present participle deliberately. In the ministry a man must continue to learn all his days. In his theological college he will have learned; all through the days of his ministry he must continue to learn. At the end of his student days a man may do either or both of two disastrous things.

I remember a thing that daunted me at the end of my first teaching year. There was in Glasgow at that time a rather good second-hand bookshop with a fairly extensive theological section. I went down to look round it one afternoon soon after the teaching term had ended. As I looked round, the shop seemed to me to be curiously well stocked with second-hand copies of the standard textbooks. Idly I took down first one volume, then another, and another and opened them. There were names written on the fly-leaf, the names of the various former owners of the books. And I found that man after man in the final year had apparently sold his textbooks the day after the final term had ended. Man after man had said in effect that he was finished with learning. I do not think that that is quite as likely to happen now. But it was a grim thought. It was as if to say that farewell to college meant farewell to study.

The second thing which can happen is at least as dangerous. It is that a man should go from his college to forget all that he has been taught there. No longer for him the adventure of thinking; no longer for him the study of the new discoveries and the new horizons which are continually emerging. He is going to settle down to the old orthodoxies and the pious conventional phrases. The tragedy is that what is taught in the classroom so seldom reaches the pulpit.

I think that the reason in a number of cases is not that the man himself does not accept what he has been taught but that he is afraid of his congregation. And although there are some in every congregation who are eager to cry heresy and to let loose the dogs of theological war, it is very often the case that the people in the congregation are eager for the new truth. I had a friend, a very distinguished minister, who, when I knew him was an old man. He had begun his ministry in a remote highland parish. One Monday morning he received a message from his senior elder that the elder would like to see him. So my friend went to the old elder's house. After the usual courtesies had been exchanged the elder said to my friend: 'Did I understand you yesterday to imply that such and such a psalm was not written by David?' My friend inwardly thought: 'This is it.' But, certain that nothing would be gained by hedging he said: 'Yes. That is so.' 'Have you good evidence for this?' said the old man. 'Do the best scholars agree with this conclusion?' 'Yes,' said my friend. And then an astonishing thing happened. The old elder rose from his seat, and my friend awaited an explosion of outraged piety. Then the old elder said: 'I thank God for this day, for I have all my life prayed that there were certain psalms that David did not write.' He was thinking of the cursing psalms with the intensity of their longing for vengeance. The people had been waiting for the truth that the preacher had hesitated to give.

I do not envy the congregation which has to sit under the man who has decided that he is released from learning the moment his college door shuts behind him, or who has nervously decided that he will seek the safety of the old orthodoxies and old conventional language.

What then must be the method of this study? George Johnstone Jeffrey, in his Warrack Lectures *The Grace Wherein We Stand*, has some interesting advice. His advice is, first, clear your desk of everything except bible, paper and pen, and for two hours consult no one. 'I am convinced,' he says, 'that the first panic-stricken rush into the arms of the waiting commentators is the death of any originality a man may possess.' He then goes on to quote certain advice which Dr Johnson gave for the study of Shakespeare:

Let him who is as yet unacquainted with the powers of Shakespeare and who desires to feel the highest pleasures that the drama can give, read every play from the first scene to the last with utter negligence of all his commentators. When his fancy is on the wing, let it not stop at correction or explanation. Let him read on through brightness or obscurity, integrity or corruption; let him preserve his comprehension of the dialogue and his interest in the fable, and when the pleasures of novelty have ceased, let him attempt exactness and read the commentators.

If you do this, Jeffrey goes on to say, 'at the end of two hours' lonely wrestling, you may feel you can inscribe the hard-won results on your thumb-nail'. But, Jeffrey holds, it is only after that lonely and direct approach that a man should turn to the great commentators.

I would not be sure about this. For most of us to turn to the text of any ancient book, and above all of the Bible, naked and unarmed, with nothing but our own resources, would be an act of intolerable and unforgivable arrogance. But even if we do begin with the direct confrontation, we must sometimes start with the great expositors. And when I say 'great' I mean great. The most fatal thing of all is to read nothing but other people's sermons—even the greatest of them—and to read nothing but the so-called 'devotional' commentaries. If there is one bit of good advice in regard to study, it is to keep always on one's desk at least one great difficult book, a book which really stretches the mind.

This is not to say that any sermon should be a parade of learning. Gossip tells how he once heard Rainy speaking with enthusiasm of a certain preacher's scholarly sermons. 'But,' someone else said, 'will the simple people to whom he preaches follow him at all?' 'Oh, well,' said Rainy, 'they will have the comfortable feeling that something very fine is going on'—'somewhat meagre fare' for the worshipper, as Gossip commented. The proverb is true of preaching as it is of so many things—Art lies in concealing art. And the thing which sounds most lucid and clear and simple may well be, will almost certainly be, the product of much study and thought, and has been made supremely understandable for others because the preacher has toiled to understand it himself. It is not the processes of his thought that the preacher must transmit, but the results of his thought, just as in a scholarly volume a score of footnotes may be necessary to indicate the sources of one limpid paragraph.

(ix) This is to say that one of the main aims of preaching must be intelligibility. I think that there are many preachers who do not realise the gap between the trained 'professional' theologian and the layman. Very recently I was a member of a little group of young theologians, who met on certain evenings to hear papers by members of the group and to discuss them. In my old age these young men did me the honour of allowing me to share their discussions. Because I wanted to see what a layman would make of the talk of a group like that, I persuaded them to ask a friend of mine to join us. This friend of mine has a long association with the Church. He was brought up in a home in which religion was a reality. He was a leading member of the Youth Fellowship in my church in Renfrew in the old days. He is a highly intelligent person. He holds the very responsible post of foreman pattern-maker in one of the great shipyards on the Clyde. He is an elder of the Church, and has been both a Presbytery and General Assembly representative elder. He is an expert musician, and a competent organist. He is a skilled photographer. He has been a leader of one of the groups who do restoration work on the lonely island of St Kilda. He is a Fellow of the Society of Antiquaries of Scotland, and his researches on interesting places find ready magazine publication. In other words, although he left school early and has no higher education Archie is a highly cultured, highly skilled, and highly intelligent person. He came to half a dozen meetings of that little

85

group, he listened, he enjoyed being there; on occasion he would make a shrewd contribution to the conversation; but time and time again on his own admission he just had no idea of what it was all about. Nothing could better show the gap between the professional theologian and philosopher and the intelligent, thinking, articulate layman. And too often the preacher loses the battle for intelligibility. Two things are constantly to be remembered.

First, there is the simple but basic fact that a sermon is heard. If you are reading a book, you can go back and read a paragraph a second or a third time, if you don't understand it at the first reading. You cannot do that with a sermon. If you are engaged in a discussion, you can cross-question the speaker. You cannot do that with a sermon. In the sports reel parts of television one of the most useful things is the replay of an exciting moment, and still better the replay in slow motion. But you cannot have a slow motion replay of a paragraph in a sermon that you did not understand. The very fact that a sermon is *heard*, not read, makes it very much more difficult to keep up with it. And if the hearer happens to miss the meaning of a sentence or two, or even if he does not hear a sentence or two correctly, then he will very probably end up faint and not even pursuing.

Second, there is the fact that, when a man gets into a pulpit, if he has done the normal course of training, he will have spent about four years listening to lectures and reading theology. He will have acquired a vocabulary, an attitude of mind, a familiarity with certain ways of thinking and speaking, all of which make listening to sermons second nature to him. The layman is not like that; he can't be.

W. E. Sangster laid the foundations of his fame as a preacher when he was in Aintree, where people flocked to his church. His son Paul Sangster in his biography of his father writes:

My mother played an important part in these services. She had to hear the sermons read aloud every Saturday morning. Any word or phrase or idea which was not immediately clear to her was struck out. At least once my father grew impatient of her slowness of understanding. 'Will,' he was told, 'you may know what you are talking about, but I don't.' 'Oh! That's the worst of these pigeon brains!' 'Yes, but remember, those will be the brains you'll be preaching to tomorrow night.' He gave in.

Sangster was abundantly right in his battle for intelligibility; he was equally abundantly wrong in his talk of 'pigeon brains'. It was simply that the ordinary man did not speak the language of the preacher or the theologian. Reverse the positions. Put Sangster, or any other preacher for that matter, in the garage, in the machine shop, in the electric repair shop, in the television repair shop, in the surgeon's theatre or the dentist's surgery, in the wholesale food market, in the chemist's, the metallurgist's or the botanist's laboratory—and he is going to be just as pigeon-brained.

And the preacher's problem is the most complicated of all. The expert in other fields does not need to make himself understood outside his own profession. I can use electricity without knowing anything about it, and without even being able to repair it; but religion is every man's business and every man must understand.

The preacher cannot assume intelligibility; he must battle for it.

(x) It is obvious that no one is going to come to listen to anyone preaching, unless that preaching is relevant. Gossip quotes a resolution of Dr Johnson, 'if I can hear the sermon to attend it, unless attention be more troublesome than useful'. Unless the listening is useful, no one is going to listen.

In the late nineteen-fifties the Methodist Home Mission Department launched an attempt at outreach to the people without much success. 'We are appalled,' said Sangster, 'by the granite indifference of the artisan masses to our faith.' There are many whose attitude it is that they can and do get on well enough without religion and that they are just not interested. It is perfectly clear that they are not going to be interested, unless they can be persuaded that religion is relevant to them and to their lives.

It is true that there are times when the charge of irrelevance is justified. There are times when the Church does seem to have a genius for stressing the irrelevant. I heard of a minister in a part of the country where the fortunes of the Church are at a very low ebb. This man was heard to say that his one ambition was to introduce Gregorian chanting before he left his parish—a country parish at that. Howard Williams tells how an Anglican friend of his came to a service in Bloomsbury, only to inform Dr Williams at the end that the service had been spoiled for him because the prayer of thanksgiving preceded any prayer of confession. Certainly correct ritual and liturgy are desirable, but when they become the main aim of the service, they have usurped a place that is not theirs.

There can be in every service of the Church a personal relevance. Gossip used to tell how after a service a man once came to him almost with tears of gratitude. Gossip said to the man: 'Would you mind telling me what in the service has moved you so much?' The man said: 'I'm an old man now. I happen to be a lawyer. And never in all my life did I hear lawyers mentioned in prayer, until you prayed for them today.' For some reason Gossip had prayed for lawyers in his intercessory prayer, and for this one man the service had come vividly alive. I have had something of the same experience. Very often, when I used to take services, in the prayer of intercession I would pray for 'those whose task it is to keep clean and sweet this place of worship'. And again and again I would find that a church officer or a church cleaner would come to say thanks that they had been remembered in prayer—a remembrance which seldom happened. At least once in a while every person in the congregation should be able to say of something in a service: 'That means me!'

There can be the demonstration by the individual Christian that his religion is relevant to his everyday life. G. ffrench Beytagh, the former Dean of Johannesburg, whose Christian witness against apartheid brought him to trial and temporary imprisonment, in his book *Encountering Darkness* tells of the experience which was influential in his conversion. He had lived a pretty erratic life. The experience which brought him to the Church happened of all times and places at midnight in a bar. He had been drinking with a man, and just about midnight he insisted that it was his turn to stand the man a drink. The man looked at his watch, and refused. Beytagh pressed him; he still refused. Beytagh was annoyed. 'Why,' he said, 'will you not drink with me?' 'It is after midnight,' the man answered, 'and I am going to make my communion in church this morning.' Beytagh was shattered. Here was a man whose drinking habits on a Saturday night were dominated by the fact that, as he saw it, he must go fasting to early morning Communion, and in an hotel bar he was not afraid to say so. This man's religion affected his life.

Many years ago now there was in Scotland a famous young international football player called Tommy Walker. Tommy Walker was a Christian, and an active Christian. Had it not been for the war, he might well have entered the ministry. A certain well-known Scottish football referee was writing about his football experiences in a Scottish newspaper. In one of the articles he said: 'When I'm refereeing a match in which Tommy Walker is playing,

I know that I have only twenty-one players to watch, not twenty-two, because Tommy would never do a dirty thing.' Here was a young man whose Christianity affected his football.

I was once present when two men were discussing a house which one of them was contemplating buying. It was a new house. The one named the builder of the house and said to the other: 'You need not hesitate to buy one of so-and-so's houses. He builds his Christianity into his houses.' Here was a builder whose Christianity affected the houses he built.

If Christianity was given this kind of relevance, that would be preaching indeed.

There is a relevance of language and of expression. It may well be that nothing has done religion more harm than the fact that it was—and often still is—wrapped up in Elizabethan language. It is worthwhile remembering that the New Testament is written in colloquial Greek; it is written in the kind of Greek the man in the street wrote and spoke in the first century. Anything less archaic than the New Testament when it was first written would be impossible to imagine. It has been said, and said truly, that, even if the New Testament lost all its religious significance, it would remain linguistically one of the most important books in the world because it is the only literary production of the colloquial Greek of the first century. Anything which makes the New Testament sound other than contemporary mistranslates it.

And this is also true of the language of prayer. We are told in the New Testament that because of what Jesus has done for us we can call God Abba (Rom. 8.15; Gal. 4.6). Abba is the word by which a little Jewish child calls his father in the family circle. It is the exact equivalent of Daddy. I am not saying that we should call God Daddy; but I am saying that if the relationship between God and men can be expressed in that word, then to talk to God in

Elizabethan English is ridiculous. You don't talk to your father in language that no one has used for the last two and a half centuries. It is often said that we should call God 'Thou' to show that he is different from men; but the actual fact is that the Bible in the AV calls man and God by the same pronoun. The Bible calls God Thou, and also says to man: 'Thou shalt not covet.' The thou's were perfectly correct in Elizabethan English. Today they are a great hindrance. Many a man is stopped praying because he does not know the language. I am not for a moment saying that we ought to pray in colloquial slang; I am saying that we should use not Elizabethan English but the best of twentieth century English.

But not only must the language be relevant; the expression of thought must also be relevant. Take one example. There has been recent discussion in Scotland as to where in the Communion service there should be included the prayer: 'Lamb of God, that takest away the sins of the world, have mercy on us.' The question is whether it should be included at all. Canon Tristram, the nineteenth century authority on the background customs of the Bible, tells how, when he was on his way out to India, the ship put in at Ceylon, and he was asked to preach. He did not speak Sinhalese, so he had to use an interpreter. He thought that he would take a subject right at the heart of the Gospel for his one sermon, and he decided to preach on the lost sheep. At the end of the sermon the interpreter said to him: 'Sir, do you mind if I say something to you?' 'No,' said Tristram, 'say what's in your mind.' 'Sir,' said the interpreter, 'are you aware that no one in this island has ever seen a sheep?' 'What did you do with the translation?' asked Tristram. 'Oh', said the interpreter, 'I turned it into a buffalo who had lost her calf!'

What is true of Ceylon is becoming true of any urbanised and industrialised society. It was so very different in

Palestine. W. D. Davis, in *Paul and Rabbinic Judaism*, quotes some figures. In the Temple in Jerusalem in official sacrifices, not counting private sacrifices at all, there were sacrificed every year 1093 lambs, 113 bulls, 37 rams, 32 goats. Therefore the lamb metaphor was vividly appropriate for Palestine. But it may well have lost its vividness today.

It may well be that relevance demands that we rephrase our religious language and restate our religious and theological metaphors, for although Jesus first preached in Palestine, if anything is true of him, it is that he is the Great Contemporary.

(xi) And lastly, there is one thing without which all preaching is ineffective, and that is sincerity, sheer honesty. There are many accents which a man may counterfeit; he may pretend to a Scots accent, a Cockney accent, an Oxford accent, a Yorkshire accent, a Welsh accent. The one accent he cannot counterfeit is the accent of sincerity.

Does this mean that I cannot preach on anything except the things which I intensely and unconditionally believe? No, it does not mean that. I can *expound* a doctrine, explain it, show its meaning, even if I myself am not sure of it. I remember reading a thing which gave me great comfort— I think it was in one of F. R. Barry's books. I had always had difficulty in repeating the Apostles' Creed, for there are items in it which I could not hold. But Barry somewhere said that the original introduction to the Apostles' Creed was not, '*I* believe', but, '*We* believe'. That is to say, when I am reciting the Creed, I am not claiming that all this is without exception *my* personal belief; but I am stating that it is the *Church's* belief, and this of course I can do. And there is no reason why I should not explain and expound all that is in it, even if it is clear that sometimes I will be talking with the accent of the heart, and sometimes with the accent of the mind.

In any event, I must be honest. A superficial skating over of a doctrine will not do. Leslie Tizzard of Carr's Lane Church died, humanly speaking, tragically too soon. In the days when he knew he was dying and when he was no longer able to preach, and listened when he could to sermons, he once said: 'I am tired of having the front of my mind tickled.' Superficial talking can neither comfort the heart nor satisfy the mind.

On the other hand, Howard Williams tells of a sermon he once listened to in Wales:

> I went one Sunday during my summer holiday to a little chapel in Cardiganshire where the service was in the Welsh language. The congregation was small, made up of people from the farms near by. The preacher was thin and pale with dark, blue marks of coal-dust deep in his face from the days when he had been a miner. His language was lovely, like the tongue of a bard and his theme was resurrection. He told us that to believe in resurrection was a wonderful thing for the fulfilment of life not yet made complete . . . for a nation struggling hopefully towards the promised land . . . And then he paused and went on quietly to tell us that there were times when a dry doubt came over him and he could not say whether he believed or not. At the close of the service, I heard that the preacher, but a little time before, had lost in this changing life his only daughter. The blow had been swift and grievous. It was this struggle with doubt which impressed so much and made it impossible to forget.

The sheer honesty, even if it was the honesty of a fight for faith, not yet victorious, was far more effective than a bland and superficial orthodoxy. Nothing can be a substitute for the accent of honesty.

The third part of the day's work has been teaching.

For the last twenty-seven years I have taught in the Divinity Faculty of the University of Glasgow. For me teaching has always been a joy. I have never felt the same terror of teaching as I did of preaching. But it does have to be said that teaching in a Divinity Faculty presents a series of problems which are all its own. In the first place, a student will not be allowed into the great majority of university classes, unless he has certain qualifications. He will need to have a Higher Leaving Certificate (in Scotland) in French to attend the degree class in French, or in Mathematics to attend the class in Mathematics. He comes to a subject with certain basic qualifications, but this is not so in Divinity. Almost always the subjects are new to him, and no agreed foundation of knowledge can be assumed. In the second place, there is no Faculty to which students come from such a range of backgrounds. When I began to teach, the degree for which students were working was the BD, bachelor of divinity degree. At that time the BD was a second degree, and a student had to have an MA before he embarked upon it. (There is no BA degree in the older Scottish universities; the MA is the first degree.) As things are now the BD has become a first degree, in which a student does one year in the Arts Faculty, taking two degree subjects, and then three years in Divinity, although some students still do an MA before they come. In addition to this there are students who are taking what are called 'modified' courses. These are older men and women, whom the Church has accepted for the ministry, but who have been something else first, and who are beginning their studies later in life. So when a teacher in the Faculty of Divinity confronts his class, there will be in font of him some—not very many— who have already taken degrees, some even honours degrees of distinction; they will be students twenty-one or twenty-two years old, and obviously as students they have experience of learning and a certain maturity of mind.

There will be in front of him students who are only one year out of school, who are eighteen or nineteen years old, and whose experience of life and learning is much less. There will be in front of him the students—not very many—who are dong the modified courses, who may be over forty years old, who have been for years engaged in trade, or industry, or one of the other professions, who may have left school at fourteen, and who have not engaged in the technical task of learning for anything up to twenty-five years. Here then the teacher in the Faculty of Divinity may well be confronted when he begins to lecture with anyone from a young first-class honours graduate in philosophy to a man of over forty who left school at fourteen. To produce material which will cover this immense range of knowledge and of experience is no easy task. And what makes it even more exciting is that in the older Scottish universities there was a tradition—still sometimes maintained—that the professor himself taught the first year. The problem of first year teaching has in recent years been even further complicated. Until very recently Scottish students in the Divinity Faculties all did the same course for the first two years. That is to say, that in every subject the teacher could count on having the student for at least two years. Very recently the course became considerably more selective, with the result that a student may take *only* the first year of any course, and not return to that department ever again. This means that somehow or other a comprehensive survey of the subject must be compressed into one year's teaching —and in such a course the problem of priorities becomes acute. In spite of all the problems there is no part of teaching that I have enjoyed more than the teaching of the first year New Testament class.

If teaching had brought its joys, it has brought its sorrows as well. I never knew what hatred was until I began to teach. Beyond a doubt the *odium theologicum,* theological hatred, the hatred of theologians is a reality. I suppose that I am one of these people who like to be liked. I am certainly one of those people who find it impossible to work in an attitude of hostility. I never encountered hatred in my home or my school or my congregation; but when I began to teach, and particularly when I began to write, and when I began to be known outside my own town, attacks began and still go on. I have been called a child of the devil, a destroyer of the faith, a traitor to Jesus Christ. I have been informed that I am destined for hell and that there are those who are praying that I may be brought to see the error of my ways. Those who disapprove of me so strongly are those who are commonly called fundamentalists or conservatives.

This is very odd when I think of my own spiritual journey. My first introduction to public speaking was in the old Young Men's Guild, somewhere about 1925. My first speech was an attack on a speaker who suggested that in Isaiah 9.6 the comma in the AV 'Wonderful, Counsellor' should be removed, and that the phrase should read 'Wonderful Counsellor'—as indeed it does in the RSV. At that time I was so conservative in my attitude to Scripture that the removal of a comma seemed to me nothing short of a sin! To this day, as a teacher, I am quite sure that the best background a student can have is a conservative attitude to Scripture, in which he knows and loves his Bible, and in which he is prepared to learn and to mature and to use and to benefit from the riches that scholarship and learning can bring to him. For me scholarship and discovery made the Bible a far greater book than ever it had been before.

One of the most wounding things is that the attacks which are made are very often made by people who have never heard me speak, who have never read a line I have written, and who almost deliberately misunderstand what I have said, or who take some statement completely out of context. I have had students come to me after their first month of classes and apologise, and when I asked them what they were apologising about, they have said that, before they came up, they had been warned against me. They had come up suspicious and defensive, but now that they knew me better, they discovered that I was not the devil incarnate after all. The kind of thing that can happen is that I once said—and I would willingly stand by the statement —that even if there is no life after death, even if it could be proved to me that there is none, I would still regard the Christian way as the best way of life, and I would still try to follow it. As a result of that, it has repeatedly been said that I do not believe in life after death.

It has always been to me a matter of deep regret that the word evangelical must in the eyes of some people always be preceded by the word conservative—a conservative evangelical. An evangelical is surely one who loves the good news of God in Jesus Christ, and I cannot see why there should be no such thing as a liberal evangelical. I think that one of the wisest things ever said is the famous saying of Herbert Butterfield in *Christianity and History*: 'Hold fast to Christ, and for the rest be totally uncommitted.' What I believe about the Synoptic Problem and the Pastoral Epistles and their authorship, and the niceties of Christology do not for one moment affect the fact that I love Jesus Christ, and that in him I have the utter assurance that God is my heavenly Father and that my sins are forgiven.

There is a paragraph in G. A. ffrench Bcytagh's *Encountering Darkness* which goes far to summing up my own conviction:

There is a very old definition of a priest as being a man who represents God to man and man to God. I think that this is true, but by 'represent' I really mean 'introduce'. Men need someone to show God to them and a priest should be able to do so from the authority of his own personal experience—not by standing behind the authority of the Church, and thinking that wearing a dog-collar makes him an expert. A priest should himself have found Jesus as saviour—to put it in the most Protestant terms. And then he should present God to people by listening to them and accepting them as God listens and accepts. He should be unflappable and unshockable, and when he is trying to help people to find their way spiritually, he should encourage them to find the way which means most to them personally, which they always know deep down in their own hearts, and then to follow it. When I try to help people in the Christian religion, I generally say to them, 'For the love of Mike, read this book, try things this way and then do come back and see me again because what I am saying may be entirely unsuitable for you. If what I have said doesn't help, then obviously I have been wrong; and there are dozens and dozens of other ways of praying, dozens and dozens of other ways of beginning to love God.'

There are, as I have already said, two quotations of which I have always been very fond: 'God has his own secret stairway into every heart.' 'There are as many ways to the stars as there are men to climb them.' Howard Williams tells us of a saying of Keri Evans. Evans was a most unusual person. He gave up a university chair in philosophy to become the minister of a little chapel in Carmarthenshire, abandoning what had every prospect of being a brilliant academic career. He was at home in the world of scholarship, and yet he was a true child of the Welsh Revival, and a regular speaker at Keswick. Yet he writes of the growing rigidity and exclusiveness of the conservative evangelicals of his day:

With regard to other children of the revival, it grieves

me that many of them have become entombed in the letter of the doctrine, and like 'little popes' condemn all who will not accept the kind of human system they cherish.

It is not that anyone wishes to say that such people are wrong; it is not that anyone wishes them to change their beliefs. What is to be desired is that no one should believe that any human being has a monopoly of the knowledge of the way to God, and a recognition of the fact that, if a man is at peace with God, if there is the reflection of Jesus on his life, and if he loves and serves his fellowmen, if he is holding fast to Jesus Christ, then that man is a Christian. I have often quoted the dimensions of the heavenly city as they are given to us in Revelation 21.16. Each side of the city, which was in the form of a square as John saw it, was, as the RSV has it, twelve thousand 'stadia'. A *stadion* was about two hundred and twenty yards; and the RSV correctly says in the margin that twelve thousand *stadia* is about fifteen hundred miles. The area of a square whose sides are fifteen hundred miles is two million, two hundred and fifty thousand square miles! There is an immense amount of room in the city of God, room for all who come. Further, the city had twelve gates, three on the east, three on the north, three on the south, and three on the west. There was a way in from whatever direction the pilgrim to it might come. Faber was right;

> There's a wideness in God's mercy,
>   Like the wideness of the sea;
> There's a kindness in his justice
>   Which is more than liberty.
>
> For the love of God is broader
>   Than the measures of man's mind;
> And the heart of the Eternal
>   Is most wonderfully kind.

I don't think that God is nearly so much interested in orthodoxy as some of his servants are.

Before I leave the teaching area there is something I would like to say about the method of teaching. A teacher can run into two opposite dangers. He can be too detailed, too academic, too arid. G. H. C. Macgregor used to tell of a New Testament professor who taught him. The professor was lecturing on John's Gospel, and after lecturing for three months four days a week he had reached the first half of the second verse of the first chapter! I have no doubt at all that it would not be difficult to find material to produce such a course of lectures on the Prologue to John's Gospel, and on the Word. But I fear that the great majority of students would have lost interest considerably before the end of the term. On the other hand, the teacher can paint with too big a brush. Every teacher knows that, if he is going to communicate at all, he must begin by being interesting, and, in the desire to maintain interest, he may do less than justice to the more technical problems. Howard Williams tells us of Liberace's self-confessed method as a musician, perhaps the most popular pianist in the world. 'My whole trick,' he says, 'is to keep the tune well out in front. If I play Tchaikovsky I play his melodies and skip his spiritual struggles. Naturally I condense. I have to know just how many notes my audience will stand for. If there's time left over, I fill in with a lot of runs up and down the keyboard.' It is possible to lecture like that—and to preach like that! Somehow the teacher and the preacher have to find the happy medium between too much and too little.

There is one other difficulty in teaching in a Divinity Faculty. Any teacher has to hold two things in balance. Part of his duty is to convey information and part of his duty is to stimulate, and even to compel, the student to think. In no Faculty is the second task so difficult as it is in the Faculty of Divinity. Many students come to study Divinity with minds already made up, and indeed in some cases closed. They do not think that their teachers should examine them; they are there to judge their teachers. What makes matters even worse is that in Scotland many a student has been preaching sometimes for years before he comes, and is preaching while he is a student. It is rather as if you allowed a doctor to practise before he had studied medicine, or a would-be surgeon to operate before he knew anatomy. The ideal would be that no student should preach until he had undergone the prescribed training. It would not be possible to legislate for that, for after all a man has a right to share his experience with those who will listen. But the best teacher in the world cannot teach the man who knows it all already; and the first essential for teaching is willingness to learn. It is a fact that the very large majority of students come in the progress of their course to learn their own inadequacy, and at the end of the day even those who originally looked on their training as an unfortunate necessity feel that it has been far too short.

And so to the last part of the day's work; and in this I take two things together—writing and broadcasting, whether on sound radio or on television.

I am quite sure that this is the most important thing I have done, and for this reason. When I was a parish minister, I had to face the fact that fewer than one in ten people came to church anyway. With nine-tenths of the people I could have very little effective contact. When I went to teach in the Divinity Faculty of the university, I had what was to a very large extent a captive audience. They had to come, or they would not satisfy the conditions that the Church laid down for entry to the ministry. What about all that tremendous mass of people outside, the people with whom I had no effective contact at all?

There have been people who have been quite content to work away with their own little circle of people. But there have been people who have been haunted by the people outside—and I have always been like that. In that magnificent biography of William Booth, *The General next to God*, Richard Collier tells a thing about William Booth. At one meeting, packed to capacity, one of his *aides* Lieut.-Col. William Haines exulted to the General: 'Wonderful, General—did you see them? A hundred to the penitent form in ten minutes!' Booth was sombre. 'I saw the hundreds going out,' he said, 'having rejected Christ.' Booth was always haunted by the man outside. When W. E. Sangster was in Aintree, so many outsiders crowded to his services that the regular members complained. 'If necessary,' said Sangster, 'I shall ask you regular members to stay away, but I must get these outsiders in.' G. A. ffrench-Beytagh tells how when he was Dean of Salisbury he tried to contact those who most needed help. He says:

It is often said that the Church is full of neurotics and hypocrites, and this is perfectly true. The Church should want them, when everyone else regards them as nuisances, and I wish the Church had more of them.

It is very unlikely that we will make real contact with the person outside the Church by way of the ordinary church services. This is no new thing. Gossip tells how Carlyle once said, 'that the Church is in danger; and truly so it is. Its functions are becoming more and more superseded. The true Church of England, at this moment, lies in the editors of its newspapers'.

Carlyle lived long before the days of radio and television; but this certainly is true—the printed word will go where the spoken word will never go. It is here that the real ecumenical movement lies. Hardly a day passes but I receive from all over the world letters about the things I have written, and far more than half the letters are from Roman Catholics and Anglicans and all kinds of Churches, speaking all kinds of languages.

What has done this more than anything else is paperback publishing. Many a man would never dream of entering a theological bookshop. But on the bookstall of a railway station or air terminal, or even at the little shop at the corner, he sees a book, idly picks it up and looks at it, is caught by something in it, buys it, and then, if he is interested, goes on to buy more and more.

In his autobiography *In and Out of the Box.* Robert Dougall has some very interesting things to say of music on the air:

> Before the war, the two domestic networks, the National and the Regional, had both carried the whole range of entertainment and information. In this way, for instance, the BBC had built up an immense following for serious music by introducing listeners to it almost by accident. A symphony concert or a piano recital might be sand-wiched between a variety show and the commentary on a football match. So tens of thousands must have come to an appreciation of classical music, simply because their sets were left switched on after the lighter and more familiar fare they had first opted to hear.

So with paperback publishing a religious book will be on the bookstall between an Agatha Christie and a Denis Wheatley. If it had been in a religious or even a general bookstore the ordinary man would never have seen it; but there he sees it by accident—and the way to another man outside has been opened. There is an opportunity here such as has never been before. The ministry of print can reach where the ministry of the voice can never penetrate.

But I will say this—the man who will write for the ordinary man must have some experience of speaking to the ordinary man. One of the things that I have most enjoyed in life and most benefited from has been extra-mural teaching. There I was faced with the task of making theology intelligible to the layman. Now that I have to give up my university teaching, I hope that I will still be allowed to do some extra-mural teaching. Anatole France spoke of a certain writer as a man who had never looked out of the window; and I am certain that if a man is going to write, he must still have the living experience of teaching.

But if the book will reach the man outside, how much more radio or television! I remember the first time I ever did a religious broadcast. It was the People's Service and Stanley Pritchard was in charge. He said to me: 'There's a man in a house in a room reading the Sunday paper. *Stop him!*' This is the challenge. Broadcasting gives a preacher the entry into millions of homes; they will certainly not come to church, but the Church has come to them. 'You become,' as Robert Dougall said, 'a privileged guest at innumerable firesides.' Robert Dougall tells how he was tested by Professor Lloyd James before his first appointment as an announcer. 'Now,' said the Professor, 'I want you to imagine that I am thousands of miles away, somewhere in the middle of the jungle, it is very hot and steamy, I am being plagued with flies, and my supply of Scotch has given out. You have to rivet my attention with the News from London.' 'He had taught me,' says Robert Dougall, 'a lesson I have never forgotten. A broadcaster in sound or vision must always work hard to hold attention. He should always remember that he is at the mercy of a switch and it is his job to ensure that the viewer or listener does not use it.'

So with broadcasting the opportunity is great, but so is the effort involved. If I had one sentence of advice to anyone who proposes to preach or teach on the air, it would quite certainly be—'Never underrate your audience.'

Nothing less than the best will do. The person who is going to listen does not want pleasant little talks or souped up children's sermons. He wants to know what the Bible is saying, and what religion is all about. The broadcaster must speak as a thinking man to thinking men.

It may well be that the future of religion lies with broadcasting. It is a strange fact that, when one broadcasts, there is no sensation of loneliness and no sensation of talking into nothing, even if there is no studio audience. Robert Dougall talks of the people, many of them lonely, who are regular listeners, and who depend on the fellowship of the air. 'The curious thing is,' he says, 'that one came to sense this companionship, and always on entering the studio I too felt among friends.' A Church of the air is not an impossible dream.

5

TESTAMENT OF FAITH

I want to end this book by setting down again the things
which I have most surely believed. I have to some extent
done so already, but I want to do it again.

I BELIEVE IN GOD
I have already said that, since I am a simple-minded person,
the argument from design, even though it is nowadays
discredited by the experts, still weighs strongly with me.
Away back in 1748 Colin Maclaurin in his *Account of Sir
Isaac Newton's Philosophical Discoveries* said succinctly:
'A manifest contrivance suggests a contriver.' And the
world is a manifest contrivance. Kant, says M. L. Clarke in
his book on Paley, did not regard the evidence from design
as sufficient in itself to prove the existence of God, but he
none the less called it 'the oldest, the clearest argument, and
that most in conformity with the common reason of
humanity'. Cicero in *Concerning the Nature of the Gods*
speaks of the orrery, the model of the solar system that
Posidonius made, a model 'which at each revolution produces the same motions of the sun, the moon and the five
planets that take place in the heavens every twenty-four
hours', and then he goes on to ask, if some one took that
orrery to Scythia or Britain, the outposts of the world,
'would any single native doubt that this orrery was the work

of a rational being?' And if so with the model, how much more with the real thing?

But not only do I believe in God; in addition to that

I BELIEVE THAT GOD CARES

I think that the best proof that God cares is the existence of the world. I think that we could argue that for the God revealed to men by Jesus Christ the act of creation was a necessity of his being. If God is love, then God must have someone to love. Love cannot exist by itself; it must go out to someone. Therefore in order to complete himself God had to create a world which he could love and which would love him. God took the risk which love always takes, the risk of rejection. If God had been only power, light, knowledge there would have been no world, because there would have been no necessity for a world; it is because God is love that God is also creator.

I am going to come back to this when I talk about belief in man, but for the moment I am going to leave it there. I believe that God is, and I believe that God cares.

I BELIEVE IN JESUS

The days when anyone could argue that Jesus was no more than myth are long past. I believe that Jesus lived and I believe that Jesus died. I don't need to depend on the New Testament solely for that. The record is there in the *Annals* of Tacitus (15.44). The *Annals* were written in AD 115–117. The mention of Jesus comes when Tacitus is dealing with the story of the great fire of Rome, which devastated the city in AD 64. The Roman populace was convinced that Nero had deliberately set the city ablaze in in order to be able to rebuild it. The fire burned for five days. Reports said that attempts to extinguish it were hindered. In some way Nero had to transfer the blame to someone else. He transferred it to the Christians. No

amount of lavish gifts and prayers and sacrifices to pro-
pitiate the gods availed 'to banish the sinister belief that
the conflagration was the result of an order'.

> Consequently to get rid of the report, Nero fastened the
> guilt and inflicted the most exquisite tortures on a class
> hated for their abominations, called Christians by the
> populace. Christus, from whom the name had its origin,
> suffered the extreme penalty during the reign of Tiberius,
> at the hands of one of our procurators, Pontius Pilate, and
> a most mischievous superstition, thus checked for the
> moment, again broke out not only in Judaea, the first
> source of the evil, but even in Rome, where all things
> hideous and shameful from every part of the world find
> their centre and become popular.

The life of Jesus in Palestine and his death under Pontius
Pilate are beyond argument.

I believe that Jesus in his life and death demonstrated
the limitless and indestructible love of God.

I believe that this Jesus so appeared to his men that they
were convinced that he had conquered death. I do not
know what exactly happened. Mary is told not to touch him
(John 20.17); Thomas is invited to touch him (John 20.27).
Sometimes Jesus is so spiritual that doors are no obstacle
to him (John 20.19,26), and he comes and goes at will
(Luke 24.31); sometimes the story is so physical that he is
depicted as claiming to have flesh and blood and is shown
eating a meal (Luke 24.36–43). But I am not worried by the
difficulties. I am certain that something happened to make
Jesus available for all time in all places to those who love
him and believe.

John Drinkwater's poem expresses precisely the way in
which Jesus differs from other great men:

> Shakespeare is dust, and will not come
> To question from his Avon tomb,

And Socrates and Shelley keep
An Attic and Italian sleep.

They see not. But, O Christians, who
Throng Holborn and Fifth Avenue,
May you not meet, in spite of death,
A traveller from Nazareth?

The others we know about; Jesus we know. The others we
remember: Jesus we experience.

I suppose that I ought to say next I BELIEVE IN THE HOLY
SPIRIT—and so I do. But to be honest, I find it very difficult
to distinguish between the Holy Spirit and the ever present
Risen Lord. It is the coming of the Spirit which is to take
away the desolation of the disciples (John 14.18). It is the
Spirit who is to remind the disciples of what Jesus had said
(John 14.26). It is the Spirit who is to convict man of his
own sin and of Jesus' righteousness (John 16.7–11). It is
the Spirit who is to bring the new truth, as men are able and
ready to receive it (John 16.12). In a fine phrase G. H. C.
Macgregor said that the Holy Spirit is Jesus Christ's
alter ego. And I think that Paul felt the same way, for he
said: 'Now the Lord is the Spirit' (I Cor. 3.17). I am content
to think of the Spirit and of the Risen Lord as one at least
in action.

I BELIEVE IN THE WORLD
The first of the great heresies, the heresy called Gnosticism,
taught that the world, and every material thing, including
the body, are evil. And it is a heresy from which the Church
has never fully escaped. The Letter to Timothy tells how
there are those who teach abstinence from marriage and
from foods, 'which God created to be received with thanksgiving by those who believe and know the truth, for every-

thing created by God is good, and nothing is to be rejected,
if it is received with thanksgiving' (I Tim. 4.3,4). For that
reason I believe that the Christian should enjoy life and
enjoy the world.

No one will deny the greatness of Puritanism, but there
are few who will deny that Puritanism's suspicion of the
world has much to answer for. John Richard Green in
The Short History of the English people says that under
Puritanism:

> Little things became great things in the glare of religious
> zeal; and the godly man learned to shrink from a surplice,
> or a mince pie at Christmas, as he shrank from the
> impurity of a lie.

Macaulay in his *History of England* writes of what happened
under Puritanism:

> It was a sin to hang garlands on a Maypole, to drink a
> friend's health, to fly a hawk, to hunt a stag, to play at
> chess, to wear lovelocks, to put starch into a ruff, to
> touch the virginals, to read the Faerie Queene . . . The
> fine arts were all but proscribed. The solemn peal of the
> organ was superstitious. The light music of Ben Jonson's
> masques was dissolute. Half the fine paintings of England
> were idolatrous, and the other half indecent.

That attitude did something to religion from which religion
has never totally recovered.

Rita Snowden passes down a story of Frank Boreham's.
Up in the moutain tops a traveller met an old priest. He
wondered what on earth the frail old man was doing there,
and asked him. 'I am seeing the beauty of the world,' the
old man said. 'But haven't you left it rather late?', the
traveller said. So the old man told his story. He was ill in
bed, near to the end. An angel came to him—was it vision or
dream? 'What have you come for?' the old man asked.

'To take you home,' the angel answered. 'And is it a beautiful world to which I go?' the old man asked. 'It is a very
beautiful world from which you come,' said the angel. The
old man had to say that he knew nothing of it, for he had
hardly ever been outside the monastery. 'Then,' said the
angel, 'I fear you will see very little beauty in the world
to which you are going.' The old man begged that he might
be granted just one more year to see the world he was leaving and the world he had never seen. His prayer was granted. 'Now,' he said, 'I am spending all my little hoard of
gold, and all the days I have left exploring this world's
loveliness.'

I believe in the world. I have enjoyed living. I agree with
Lizette Woodworth Reese's poem:

> Glad that I live am I;
> That the sky is blue;
> Glad for the country lanes,
> And the fall of dew.
>
> After the sun the rain,
> After the rain the sun;
> This is the way of life,
> Till the world be done.
>
> All that we need to do,
> Be we low or high,
> Is to see that we grow
> Nearer the sky.

Many years ago now I used to hear the boys and girls
singing these verses in Sunday School—and the shorter the
time left to me the more I agree with them.

I have just said that I believe in enjoying life, but at the
same time I BELIEVE IN WORK. It is the plain fact that

performances which look as if they were done effortlessly are in fact the product of the most concentrated and lengthy toil. Paderewski was one of the greatest pianists in the world, and one of the hardest practisers in the world. It was nothing for him to play a bar or a phrase of music forty or fifty times before a performance, so that he would get it just right. He once played before Queen Victoria. 'Mr Paderewski,' she said, 'you are a genius.' 'That may be,' answered Paderewski, 'but before I was a genius I was a drudge.' When Gary Player plays golf it looks easy to hit the ball two hundred and seventy-five yards down the middle of the fairway. But in practice he hits literally thousands of balls, hour after hour. He said that a golfer who did not practise was like a business-man who never went to his office, and then wondered why his business was not flourishing. Horace, the famous Roman poet, used to advise authors to keep what they have written beside them for nine years, before they published it. Thomas Gray began his famous *Elegy* in 1742 and not until 1750 was it shown even to friends. Plato's *Republic* begins with the simple sentence: 'I went down to the Piraeus yesterday with Glaucon, the son of Ariston, that I might offer up prayer to the goddess.' It is said that he wrote and rewrote that simple sentence more than a dozen times to get the form and cadence just right.

I do not believe that any great thing was ever done easily. I believe in work.

I BELIEVE IN MAN

In spite of everything that can be said I believe in the essential goodness and nobility of man. And so did Jesus. In the Gospels Jesus flings his staggering commands and demands at men—and obviously expects them to pick themselves up and to try to obey.

I believe in man because I believe that God needs men.

In some of his writings George Bernard Shaw comes very near to thinking of a struggling or an experimenting God, who needs man's help in the struggle and when things go wrong. In the early play *The Shewing-Up of Blanco Posnet* Shaw tells the story of how Blanco Posnet, the disreputable horse-thief, who was proud of being a bad man, risked his life and liberty to try to save the sick child of an unknown woman. 'God,' says Blanco, 'plays cat and mouse with you. He lets you run loose until you think you're shut of him, and when you least expect it he's got you.' So Blanco preaches his 'sermon' about what happened to himself and Feemy the loose woman in regard to the sick child.

> What about the croup? It was early days when He made the croup, I guess. It was the best He could think of then; but when it turned out wrong on his hands He made you and me to fight the croup for him. You bet he didn't make us for nothing; and he wouldn't have made us at all if He could have done his work without us. By Gum, that must be what we're for! He'd never have made us to be rotten drunken blackguards like me, and good-for-nothing rips like Feemy. He made me because He had a job for me. He let me run loose till the job was ready; and then I had to come along and do it, hanging or no hanging. And I tell you it didn't feel rotten; it felt bully, just bully. Anyhow, I got the rotten feeling off me for a minute of my life; and I'll go through fire to get it off me again.

Here we have the extraordinary thought of an experimenting God who needs men to correct his mistakes.

In another essay entitled 'The Infancy of God', never published until Warren Sylvester Smith published it in *Shaw on Religion* in 1967, he talks about 'the idolatry which conceives of God as perfect and omnipotent'. 'How are atheists produced?' he demands.

In probably nine cases out of ten, what happens is something like this. A beloved wife or husband or child or sweetheart is gnawed to death by cancer, stultified by epilepsy, struck dumb and helpless by apoplexy, or strangled by croup or diphtheria; and the looker on, after praying vainly to God to refrain from such horrible and wanton cruelty, indignantly repudiates faith in the divine monster, and becomes not merely indifferent and sceptical, but fiercely and actively hostile to religion.

The person cannot understand how an omnipotent God, a God who could have stopped that, allowed it to happen, and so is driven to the conclusion that, if God is omnipotent, he cannot be good. But—and here is the point—God is not the omnipotent God, he is the struggling God. 'In the old times, God was not really conceived as omnipotent, but as the divine antagonist of a malign power which wrestled with him for the souls of men.' And just as when the Devil wants a man to do something for him, he tempts the man, so does God. Then God becomes dependent on the man, And so when a man becomes a temple of the Holy Spirit, and therefore the agent of the Holy Spirit, the man is also necessarily the limitation of the Holy Spirit, God is, as it were, in his infancy. He fights his battle with the cosmic adversary, and his weapon is man, man with all his limitations.

It may be heresy, but there is something tremendous in the thought of a God who is fighting the battle of the universe, and who has deliberately made himself dependent on men. So with all my heart I believe in man.

That is why I like Robert Dougall's personal prayer. In his autobiography *In and Out of the Box*, he writes:

On some evenings when the news was more than usually grim I would nip off to the dingy dressing room opposite the studio and make a quick prayer which I had thought up to the mysterious God who pervades all life and in whom I put my trust:

> Dear Lord, may I become as unto an empty vessel, fit, in some small measure, to receive thy spirit, so that in my public and private life I may at least reflect the good and, in time, given courage and strength, may my actions come to be more pleasing in thy sight.

If it is true, as I believe it is, that God needs me, I can say Amen to that prayer.

I BELIEVE IN LOVE: I BELIEVE IN MARRIAGE: I BELIEVE IN THE FAMILY: I BELIEVE IN HOME.

I believe in love and I believe in marriage. I have never been able to see or to agree that celibacy and virginity are superior to marriage. In one sense and from one point of view they are far easier than marriage, because they have dispensed with the problem of living together. I know well that those who undertake celibacy or virginity may live in community, but life in community does not present the problem of living together in the crises and the trifles of day-to-day living. Celibacy and virginity do present one problem—the problem of dealing with the sex instinct; but that is a self-manufactured problem which should never have arisen. Sex is part of life and the deliberate annihilation of it is not a virtue; it is a criticism of life as God made it and meant it to be.

I believe that the Psalmist was profoundly right, when he said as the AV has it: 'God setteth the solitary in families' (Ps. 68.6). I believe that the old creation story made no mistake in hearing, when it heard God say: 'It is not good that the man should be alone' (Gen. 2.18). In his *One Volume Bible Commentary* William Neil comments on Genesis 2.24: 'Therefore a man leaves his father and his

mother and cleaves to his wife, and they become one flesh'—
'True marriage is beautifully described as an unselfconscious
relationship, where a man and a woman find that they have
become part of each other, almost as if they became a joint
personality.' And the joint personality which emerges is
greater and fuller than either single personality. And Jesus
took this ancient saying into Christianity also (Matt. 19.5;
Mark 10.7). I think that the ancient commentators were
right, when they suggested that the *two or three* in Jesus'
saying, 'Where two or three are gathered in my name, there
am I in the midst of them', means *father, mother and child.*

I cannot help remembering Aristophanes' speech in
Plato's *Symposium*, the dialogue in which Socrates thinks
of love. This is how A. E. Taylor summarises it in his book
Plato, the Man and his Work:

In the beginning man was a 'round' creature, with four
arms and four legs and two faces, looking different ways,
but joined at the top to make a single head. There were
originally three 'sexes', if we can call them so, of these
creatures, the double-male, the double-female, and the
male-female, the first derived from the sun, the second
from the earth and the third from the moon, which is at
once a 'luminary' and an 'earth'. But as yet there was
no sexual love and no sexual generation. The race pro-
created itself by a literal fertilisation of the soil. These
creatures were as masterful as they were strong and
threatened to storm heaven or blockade it, as we learn
from the old traditions about the 'giants'. As a measure
of safety, Zeus split them longtitudinally down the
middle and reconstructed them so that the method of
propagation should henceforth be sexual. Since then, man
is only half a complete creature, and each half goes about
with a passionte longing to find the complement and
coalesce with it again. The longing for reunion for the

lost half of one's self is what we call 'love', and, until it is satisfied, none of us can attain happiness. Ordinary wedded love between man and woman is the reunion of one of the orginally double-sexed creatures; passionate attachment between two persons of the same sex is the reunion of the halves of a double-male or double-female, as the case may be.

So this myth in vivid pictorial form has in it the truth that we cannot be complete until we find the person whom we must really and truly love, because he or she is the other half of ourself. And so the only truly happy man is the man who seeks and finds the other half of himself. This is not to say that the two partners who have found each other will never differ, never argue, never even quarrel and sometimes fight. But it does mean that, even when they are having their most violent differences, there is no one in the world with whom they would rather be.

I BELIEVE IN THE CHURCH

Maybe it is fitting that I who have served the Church for more than forty years should end up by saying, I believe in the Church. I can remember no time in my life when the Church was not part of my life. I am not unaware that the membership of the Church is shrinking from year to year. I am not unaware that, although it is possible to point to churches which are crowded, they are few and far between, and the average congregation is becoming smaller, older and more female all the time. I am not unaware that there are many people who are genuinely religious, and who yet find nothing in the Church. Robert Dougall writes of the way he felt when he was a young man:

About this time, I began to feel disenchantment with Sunday church-going. There was no Welfare State and social inequalities and hardships were great. The Church

didn't seem to be doing much about it. To my eyes, the
Bishop and the Vicar began to look smug and well-fed.
The congregation was almost wholly middle-class; and I
felt the Church had lost touch with life . . . At no time
did I cease to believe in the deity, but I couldn't feel near
him in church. For me God was in the woods and fields
and changing seasons.

And I think that there are genuinely many in that same
position, even more of them than when Robert Dougall was
a young man. To some extent I can see why.

First, the problem today is not hostility to the Church;
it is indifference. For many the Church is simply irrelevant;
it is not even worth criticising, it is simply to be ignored.
Rita Snowden, who loves the Church, wrote a book called
When We Two Walked in which she tells of her experiences
on a walking tour in the south of England. One Sunday she
and her friend came to an ancient and lovely village church,
and went in to worship there. She describes the service:

> It was all very simple. There couldn't have been more
> than twenty people besides the Vicar and the organist
> and ourselves. The little choir of three lead the con-
> gregation out on dignified adventures of song, but all with
> such gentleness that, but for one soprano and an uncer-
> tain bass four seats away, the old church was not greatly
> disturbed. Hymn and psalm and prayer, and the quiet
> murmuring voice of the Vicar tended to take my thoughts
> out of the windows into the morning sunlight and over the
> fields and far away. The pity is, it was all so harmless,
> so gentle, so proper. There was nothing about it, save
> perhaps the beautiful language in which the prayers were
> couched and the reading of Mark's Gospel to remind one
> of that Young Man who strode the countryside and
> talked with the country people of Galilee, in burning
> words.

The pity is—the pity is that the Church can be so harmless that it would not be worthwhile to take the trouble to crucify it.

Second, the Church characteristically and constitutionally dislikes change. Tennyson had it that God fulfils himself in many ways 'lest one good custom should corrupt the world'. So often the Church has clung on to a good custom until that good custom became a handicap and a millstone. George Bernard Shaw had things to say about this. He wrote in the 1920s an article entitled 'A Note on the Prayer Book', when Prayer Book revision was in the air. He held that the Book of Common Prayer is based on a universe which is 'not merely pre-Einsteinian but pre-Newtonian, not merely pre-Newtonian but pre-Copernican'. It has therefore, says Shaw, 'no place in modern religious thought'. Then he goes on:

> Frankly, the book is worn out. It is past repair. And if and when a new one is established by Act of Parliament a clause should be added making revision compulsory every six years at most. I have said elsewhere that the law of change is the law of God; and the Churches which deny this and try to keep their hold on the people by rituals stereotyped for eternity will presently find their already quarter-filled temples quite empty.

Whether or not we agree with the verdict of Shaw on the Book of Common Prayer we cannot dispute that the law of change *is* the law of God. In another article, also written in the 1920s, entitled 'On Ritual, Religion and the Intolerableness of Tolerance', Shaw returned to the attack, 'Any Church,' he says, 'which makes a great fuss when a cathedral pillar sinks or a wall cracks, and collects a great sum to have the building under-pinned and made safe, but sees its creeds and services going crazy with age, and sinking and rifting and tumbling in all directions without saying a word about them except to swear that they are as safe as the pyramids, and that those who are complaining that they will presently fall and bury the nation in their ruins are disreputable liars, that Church will end, as many churches have ended in England, in having buildings without congregations.' Unless a Church speaks to men and to God in contemporary language, and with a full realisation of its contemporary background of science and culture, no one will listen to it. True, there is an unchanging gospel, but that gospel has to be interpreted to meet the need of each and every age.

Third, there is a sense in which the Church is too careful, too polite and too unwilling to give offence. Hugh Carleton Greene the director of the BBC said in 1965 in a speech in Rome to the International Catholic Association for Radio and Television certain things which are true, as Robert Dougall tells:

> I believe we have a duty to take account of the changes in society, to be ahead of public opinion rather than always to wait upon it. I believe that great broadcasting organisations, with their immense power of patronage for writers and artists, should not neglect to cultivate young writers who may by many be considered 'too advanced', even 'shocking'.

The he went on to say: 'Provocation may be healthy and indeed socially imperative.' There is a duty to be provocative and that duty the Church has by no means always faced.

June Bingham put at the very beginning of her biography of Reinhold Niebuhr, *Courage to Change*, a prayer which Neibuhr himself wrote and used:

> O God give us
>> Serenity to accept what cannot be changed,

Courage to change what should be changed,
and Wisdom to distinguish the one from the other.

And that is no bad prayer for the Church.

And so to the end—and if I were to begin life over again,
I would choose exactly the same service.